T0294273

The Little Hours
New and Selected Poems

The Little Hours

New and Selected Poems

Hilary Llewellyn-Williams

SEREN

Seren is the book imprint of
Poetry Wales Press Ltd.
Suite 6, 4 Derwen Road, Bridgend, Wales, CF31 1LH
www.serenbooks.com
facebook.com/SerenBooks
twitter@SerenBooks

The right of Hilary Llewellyn-Williams to be identified as
the author of this work has been asserted in accordance
with the Copyright, Designs and Patents Act, 1988.

© Hilary Llewellyn-Williams, 2022

ISBN: 9781781726624
Ebook: 9781781726631

A CIP record for this title is available from the British Library.

The publisher acknowledges the financial assistance of the Books Council of Wales.

Printed in Bembo by 4Edge Ltd, Hockley

Contents

New Poems

For Michael

from The Tree Calendar

If You Should Come To My House

If you should come to my house
warm with walking in the cold dusk
of the afternoon, walking quickly,
being far too impatient to catch the bus,
to arrive at last all windswept at my door
with your white breath about you, if
you should knock suddenly
while I was making coffee just for
one, or cleaning out my cluttered room
in readiness for a chance visitor like you,
I'd run to meet you down every stair;
I'd fling my door wide to you, and soon
you would be sitting here
with my coffee in your hands, the whole place
in a muddle, but music on, and you'd feel
the fire's warmth on your face;
just supposing that you should come
out of the blowing leaves and autumn smoke
bright copper in the dropping sun, out
of the wind to my house and to my room
I would never turn you out into the rain:
I would greet you with a smile and take your coat,
happy to sit you in my one chair,
and never shut my eyes to you again.

Deathday

for my grandmother, d. April 1972

She lay cupped in white pillows
between purity of sheets
like a virgin laid in her snow;
her skin fine with a feathery softness
clinging gently to bones
at rest, her hands grained and veined
beautiful, her empty breasts
thin and small and hidden.
Brown eyes still bright she lay
watching the shifting colours of the world
tremble and dim, the humming
of voices mingled and spilled into dream;
she was waiting alone in the white sheath
of her body quietly with the quietness
of years, waiting
for strength to close her eyes against the sky,
courage to rebel against the blood,
for power to unclench the heart's hold;
patient to await the fires that would
submit her to the motions of the earth
that moved to bring her forth.

Day Beginning

This morning, warm and sleepy, wearing
the sun alone we lay tousled
and tender, motionless
but for slow motions of hands passing over and over
lazily, lighter than dust;
lying so close on the crumpled bed
where night had been hot
and clumsy, we caressed
without heat in the pure
light from the windows. Still the faint
sweat-scent, sweet and salt on sheets
and skin, but fading; wideawake
yet clasped by sleep were we quiet-breathing
and aware. Time and the golden
morning ticked away. Cool and smooth
our bodies reflected the patterns of the sun,
our minds without fear or fever reflected
each other: no past, no future,
we lay at the beginning of our day.

Breadmaking

Forgive the flour under my fingernails
the dabs of dough clinging to my skin:
I have been busy, breadmaking.
So easy, the flakes falling feathery
into the warm bowl, as I dip and measure
and pour the foaming treasured brown
yeast down to the ground wheat grain.
O as the barm breaks and scatters
under my working fingers like a scum
of tides on shifting sands, the secret cells
swell, you can smell their life
feeding and beating like blood
in my bunched palms
while I lift the lump and slap it back again.

It moves, like a morning mushroom,
a breathing side, stirring, uncurling
animal roused from sleep; so I pummel
and thump and knuckle it into shape
to see it unwind like a spring,
soft as a boneless baby on the table.
I have covered it now: let it grow
quietly, save for the least rustle
of multiplication in the damp bundle
telling of motion in the fattening seeds.
Its body's an uproar as I open the burning door –
It gives one final heave, and it blossoms out
To the brown loaf I have spread for you.
Taste the butter melting its heart like snow.

When My Baby Looks At Trees

for Rowan

When my baby looks at trees he sees
the wind's shape;
his face becomes still
as the branches sway and dip
for his delight, as the bright
sky dances through. He stares,
his nose twitches at leaf
and resin, sour bark, sweet earth,
the juices in the wood.

If he could climb trees
he'd be out of my arms and up
in the creaking heights
laughing among the leaves;
and his white hands move jerkily
trying to touch. What he sees
is the glow of the sap as it spreads
out and upwards, the shine
of the tree's breath.

His eyes widen and darken
and lighten to green;
a smile brushes his mouth
and cheek, and a look
passes light between him and the tree.
He is close in my arms, but apart.
When we turn to go
his skin smells of forests, he holds
his face to the wind.

The Song of Blodeuwedd on May Morning

Skilful woman am I
And dancing woman am I
Turning and turning on the green
Skin of the dawn fields;
Woman of light am I, my morning eyes
Too clear, too bright for you.

With calmness, with care,
With breastmilk, with dew,
My web I weave,
My spell I cast on you.

With calmness, a still point
That the world spins around
I am pulled up out of the ground,
My spell has found you.

Beauty above and below me,
Beauty behind and before me,
Beauty surrounds me –
And I sound, I resound like a drum.
I am making my magic, my power:
Flying woman who soars to the sun
Am I, lovely Goddess woman
Covered in rainbows, in feathers, in flowers.
Dark my mind with visions of stars
Of the night I have seen, where I have been:
See! I have chosen you.

Strong young man, a man of trees,
Of river-shadows, of hills, of horns;
All new and secret, my moon-mate,
I await you on the cold breeze
That brings you to me stumbling warm
From your bed, O yes with care,
With milk and with dew
I draw you to me on my white thread.

When you hear my voice, my cry,
When you see the oak blossoming
When you feel the owls pass by
Fetch your staff and run from your door –
It is I, woman of flowers, who calls,
Who holds wide her wings for you.
With beauty behind, with beauty before;
With calmness, with care,
With breastmilk, with dew
This stone I place: I bathe my face
And I wait for you.

Letter To My Sister

for Anabel

It is summer where you are, but I am cold
as I write this, and my house is dark all day,
and the garden soaks up rain like a black sponge.
You will spend Christmas, you say,
trekking the mountain roads and the coast paths
with that giant man of yours. I picture you
lean and brown, frowning into the sun,
shouldering your pack with the supple grace
I loved. I can see your face
clear as light, open as day: sunshine
is true to you. The flowers are strange
where you live, they speak Maori names
like the knock of wood on wood;
the birds crack words in your primeval trees.

I catch a dream of you, and here it is,
your blue note through my door. Pressed
in the thin folds like a paper flower
you wave to me, you sound your brand-new vowels
inflecting to the page-end, quick and small.
I look for more of you, and raise my eyes
to the far edge of the world. Down there,
beneath the roar of oceans, where the stars
make different shapes, where summer is,
lives someone that I knew in the cold wind
that blew along my shore. And as I turn
towards the sun, so she recedes
into the dark. My sister in the skin,
circling with the earth, keep good your seasons.

The Tree Calendar

Birch
December 24th – January 20th

After Twelfth Night comes the reality
of winter. When the greenery's stripped down
it's barefaced, blowing under the door.
Mean days dragging out a fraction more
before dark, make our myth of spring
ridiculous. I walk out into the stark
endless moment of January.

Old snow slumps in the hedge,
stretching the fields
wet to the birchwood, raw
black tangle against the grey.
Mud ruts, brown ice under my boot
snaps and seeps as I trudge up
to the sad ranks of trees, the thin
skin birches in their thaw.

These brittle twigs swept clear of leaves
whipping along the light,
points of dark bud concealing green,
I'll tie a bundle to my broom, for flight:
no shelter here, the rain falls through
this frostwood, the sky stares between.
The bramble jags, the stag horns of the scrub
bad musk of leafmould, in the dusk
that stirs behind my shoulder.

Birch stems lean to the loud stream
crowding beneath the wind,
thrashing their rods at winter stumps,
at the cracked, dimwit days.
Think of the woods brushed with a green haze.
Think of the covered hills
filling with cleaner light, and a gap

in the clouds for something to glance through.
I stoop in a cold shade
gathering twigs for a journey.

Rowan
January 21st – February 17th

Bride put her finger in the river
On the feast day of Bride
And away flew the hatching-mother of the cold.
                            (Carmina Gaedelica)

The roaring is loud and brown.
I hold water in the cup of my hand
it warms to my touch like blood

but I dare not put my feet to the flood:
I would be swept in the coils
of serpents and rolled to the sea.

Rain blows its feathers around me:
it tickles my face, quickens my skin.
Here is where I came down

this steep bank from a dark town
full of winter, to find the world
at a turning point. And here

I climb upwards from the sheer
rainwet drop, and I'm full of moon
and movement. Cautiously

I rest my fingers on a rowan tree
for a wand and a brand to avert
evil, a tree that's spun
full of fire, with the swelling sun
in its stubby black bud
and I've broken a twig clean;

inside it is sweet and green,
promising bundles, clusters of red.
A word said: and a bird flown.

Ash
February 18th – March 17th

Why is the ash the tree of quickening,
this month of green spikes with an early sun
shining straight in our eyes? What has it got
to do with birds' wings or the snowdrop's spark?

Its blunt shut buds are stubborn, not a crack
open, though the willow's tipped with silk:
it stays the same dull grey from the first day
of Lent till the first of May, while the earth

turns green around it. Ash is a strange tree,
coloured like cold water, and inside
sea-grained, close-rippled; but it burns
hot, fresh or dry. The bark so thin

and fine as skin, reminding me of horses.
All ash-lore, ash-mythologies run through
my mind in twisted threads. A wizard god
hung from his heels like some marauding crow

hoping to fill his brilliant emptiness
with consciousness, with webs of poetry.
Since then, we've lost our art of memory,
dismembered like the god. So I must go

to try that ancient weird hypothesis:
to learn the source of summer from the tree
in my own garden; which seems stark and still,
until I slide my hands down its smooth flank

and feel it shiver. In the encircled heart
something vibrates from skin to shin – and how

those blackstopped boughs curve upwards into blue,
fingering the invisible stars of spring!

The tremor travels down a million stones
to the muffled pulse of water. As all worlds
are tangled in its branches, so are we,
linked by the fibre fluids of the tree.

Ash breathes beneath my hands; it's full of tension,
ready to bound away with our next gale,
galloping in the hedge. And at its foot
something spins webs. I have remembered now.

Alder
March 18th – April 14th

Bwlchwernen – the alder pass.
The world swoops west,
tilts valley and hill
to the sudden light of spring,
the long, brushed shadows.

Water shines from the fields.
A brimful river sweeps
roots of alder, leaving
the rolled corpse of a lamb
to bob in the shallows.

Up here, in a stone barn
this Easter, a straggle
of children and adults saw
the outlawed story retold
of an old resurrection:

a grain reborn as a child
(as we sat in the straw):
a lost child fostered and found
to be wizard of poets, a star
with the wind's protection.

Out in the yard, our cars
mud-axled, we dispersed,
turned away from the scene.
Now I visit my alder stream
in a double life, knowing

that nothing's been lost. A raven
croaks *Brân* overhead:
banished westwards, but still
surviving. And alder flowers
green as thieves, still growing.

Willow
April 15th – May 12th

One spring I came to an unlucky place.
I carried love in a bundle on my back
and I stepped over the brink of an adventure,
wide-open, foolish. The house was dark
and nervous; the ground around
was full of willows. Their poison entered me
like swallowed water, easily.

They leaned, pollarded knobs along the stream
with witches' raised hair.
They thickened the air with something invisible:
the clay, too, was clogged with it.
Their long-flint leaves rubbed quietly
together. All the way to the edge
of the sky stood dead elms, bleached
to bone, like a winter landscape.

The corpse elms leached their deaths into the soil
and the willows bloated
drawing pain like a poultice, sucking grief
from abandoned farms and a spoilt, lumpy land
awaiting an expansion of the town
with new roads leading nowhere.
There I felt cursed: my head swum

in the sunken garden, and my energies
trickled into the mud. Mosquitos swarmed.

Now I can love willows again, in a wild
country. Their silver softens the hedge;
their gold attracts early bees.
When I touch their stems, they tremble.
But in the wind they winnow secretly:
and I'm wary of a power that drags at me
as the moon drags the seas.

Hawthorn
May 13th – June 9th

May's out: white, plump and plush
way-marker, sweet female unlucky spray;
tucked starry flowers, a million eyes
road-watching, field-guarding, a hilltop
presence, yearly more curved
with each twist of the earth, deep musk,
queen of long dusk, sharp secrets, she'll
turn to blood in the hedge, rich burning
drops. Jets leap and scream
through a damaged sky; my skin
darkens in so much light. The tightening
drum. The hum of silage cutters
from a far field, muffled by bushy May.
Smother those savage thorns
in green and white: she will be beautiful.
In a changed world, still she draws you,
enters you, as woman to woman;
and you are not hurt, but healed and washed
clean, even now, wise-eyed, reborn.

Oak
June 10th – July 7th

I put my head in the bag of leaves
and breathed green. Coarse sourjuiced crushed

smell of wet summers, that sharp male taste:
foliate-faced I sucked green with each breath,
spaced-out on oak. The fine drenching rain
felt seasidey. We walked the gleaming lane
that ribbons from hill to hill, slowly, dodging
odd Sunday cars, to our knees in tangled stalks,
flowering grasses, red cloverheads weighed down
with so much wet, the ditches murmuring.

Wine from oakleaves is tawny, tastes dark
and woody, midsummer evening fires, the sweet
smoke of peat. It is strong, climbs down deep
and blazes. It comes from the young growth:
the tender pink-flushed clusters of new leaf
offer themselves at a touch, break free
in showers of droplets, stalked green and sapped
like frankincense. You pour boiling water
on the stripped leaves: they smell of fresh tea.
The brew is bitter and brown: it could cure leather.

I sipped at last year's wine; thought, from now on
the nights draw in. This season's prime lay
stewed in a bin, filling our house with summer.
(I'm autumnal, best in receding light
in the dark half of the year). Next day
I strained the stuff, added yeast and sweetness,
set the warm juice to work. Those clear green leaves
are bloodless now, bleached out: I have
their essence bottled up, breathed in, elixir of all
oaks in me, as the sun inches south.

Holly
July 8th – August 4th

Here in high summer, holly sets fruit
that will ripen come Christmas.
Its prickles gloss and crackle in the sun.
Those deathless leaves make holly king.

This tree is holy, but not kind. What
is this holiness? What gift of grace
is so sharp-edged, dark-branched, hedged
with superstition, crowned with thorn?

Last summer's holly scratched my small
son as he climbed a bank, from rib
to breastbone a long stripe, with beads
of berry-blood, a flaxen Christ, arms up

and crying. This summer's rain
has blighted our best crops; but the trees
thrive, the trees take precedence. Green
under grey skies: reign of wood and water.

As the days shorten, holly's power grows:
ripening power, birth power, power
from behind the eyes, dream-power, spear-
leaved and bitter-barked and full of berries.

Holly saplings under graveyard yews
like prongs of resurrection, spring
from the shadows. The yews red-fleshed
and folded secretly, gave birth to them.

Blood mixed with soil was the old way
harvests grew fat, and holly ruled the feast.
My torn child heals: a ragged silver line
across his breast, fades as he flourishes.

Hazel
August 5th – September 1st

After last night's rain
light gathers on hazel leaves
with their three-clumped nuts;
and a wide-angled sun
shapes precise hills and stones.

I drag my hand through water.
Cresses stroke my skin,
which shrinks from their fleshiness.
I cup, and scoop to drink
what runs through my fingers.

A cold, sweet-metal taste:
water reflected on stone.
Myself reflected in water
shadowed and blurred, a dark
disturbance within the pool.

Tendrils of water spill down
inside me, tracing cool paths.
I splash my forehead and lids,
and wish for knowledge, for solid
sense, for a way through.

Knowledge and clarity
I need so much; I've let so much
slip by. In a hidden place
there's a well with my face in it,
smudged silver, flickering,

and hazels growing thick
overhead: and there
my eyes look out from depths
of past and future, watching
the hazel ripples lift and spread.

Bramble
September 2nd – September 29th

The smell of heaped-up blackberries in a bowl.
I am caught, small, in a rough dusty lane
leading to pinewoods, to a shining lake,
and the burnt house on the hill.
Hot full September smell: years beyond years
polish the ripening woods to gold, to falls
of chestnuts by the school, clutches of sudden

mushrooms (Do Not Touch), and scarlet
hawthorn, evening fires, and blackberries.

The trouble we had to pick them! Scrambling
up banks and over fences, into rotting ditches,
stung, scratched, tousled, burred –
yet spurred on by the purple on our tongues
and promised heaps of sweetness.
We trampled secret ways to the best clumps
through willow-herb and nettles, crouched
in a den with arching thorny stems
above us, counting our store.
That powerful, smoky fragrance. Those big
ripe berries, soft with sour blood
I sucked from my reddened fingers.

Brambles and brambles, season after season
straggle and tangle, whip out new shoots
to flower and fruit. Each year
whole families desert their cars to look
at hedgerows and waste thickets, reach
into thorns for pleasure. The plain sight
of blackberries is irresistible. It wakes
our stone-age lust for scrounging, scrumping, till
we seem to be on nature's side again,
drawn in, intoxicated; while the dark
juices of memory ferment and rise,
and I, by a ruined house, gather my treasure.

Ivy
September 30th – October 27th

In the dawn fields, white fogs lie breathing,
        making a Chinese landscape –
the Nine Kings of the North Pole descend.

Cattle shifting in the near distance
        sidle away from winter:
step by step, it has surrounded them.

The trees look thinner in this long sun:
        drawing their juices in, they
contemplate dark traceries of mould.

Brown and gold brushstrokes over the hills.
        A smell of frost and woodfires:
ivy increasing as the leaves fall.

Flowering ivy for the late bees
        full blown and glossy, tightens
its massive grip, defies the cold Kings,

keeping slow but certain purposes:
        enveloping the whole world
in patterned mounds of vegetation.

Here is a ruined cottage, sprouting
        leaves, snake-stemmed and rustling:
part of the woods now, splitting apart.

The roof gone, how can the structure stand?
        Ivy has loosened its knots.
Stone by stone, it is undone again.

From a roost above the fallen hearth
        an owl calls in full daylight:
the Nine Kings of the North Pole descend.

But they step down from whatever heights
        they journeyed in, with keen joy,
trailing blue air, a ripened sun.

There is a large fruit, still uneaten.
        Look through a crack in the door.
Nine Kings treading ivy on the floor.

Reed
October 28th – November 24th

A wind rises up
from the wetlands,

carries the cry of the sea
in deepening gusts to my door.
I draw in my head, snail
in a stone shell, doubtfully.

Southwest sunset
catches the trees, splays
out their shapes like spread
nerves, webbed and strung
vessels of drowsy fluid,
warming dull stalks to a richer
brown, until the wind lifts heavy
wings and all colours
flatten out. A long note
sounds from our chimney: winter's flute,

blowing from the throats
of reeds in the waste ground
down by the river. The dead
once fished there, dragged their nets,
crouched in the sedge for duck
and plover, stole eggs in spring.
They sheltered under reeds
in these sodden hills;
reed roofs and low stone walls
tucked down to earth,
shut in from the flapping light.

Our fenlands, wastes,
moors, marshes, and wild sloughs
are shrunken now, ploughed-up –
but give them time. Decay
puts out its tendrils. Water
seeps upwards patiently.
Stands of reeds sing
high from behind clenched teeth,
knot their roots tight,
bow to the seasons, keep firm
and yielding. Lost souls
glint from the shallows.

All night the gale
scuds over us. Dawn
will be more naked still:
the trees will be peeled sticks.
I close my eyes and pull
the covers up, but lie
aware of blind movements:
small shift of the house
downwards, the closing in
of winter, thread of roots
through water – and here's
that noise again: that shrill
dark reedy whistling.

Elder
November 25th – December 23rd

Elder in its own season –
the old dregs of the year –
is utterly empty, surely the worst
tree in the hedge, stripped dead,
gnarled and twisted afflicted
sticks, like some crabbed arthritic
witch, pale driftwood blown
inland by the gale, to catch
grotesquely by its twigs; only force
of will can colour it now thick with fruit,
or remoter still, cream-flowered,
smelling of days past, days of promise, summer.

Tree of death of all trees,
all plants; elder from Hell
(that twilight country under the hill
or holy well), where Mother Holda shakes
her feather pillows out, and we have snow.
Elf-tree: avoid it after dark
and in the dark of the year, lurking
place of the Huldre-folk, who look fair
enough, but whose backs are hollow

as stumps, damp cavities; and still
they dance on the bare margins of our world.

This wine has all the weight
of fruit in it: weight of long days,
sticky and rich with iron, blood
sour with memory. It soothes my throat.
I picked those berries in another time,
a sunlit day, with women
I no longer see. The elderberries hung
like grapes; their branches sagged,
snapped as we tugged them free: three
women under the green eye of the hill,
that massive mound built by the elder
tribe, the dark ones, thieves and dancers.

The world has tilted far
from the sun, from colour and juice.
I am tired. I draw myself in
from what's happening out there
in the rain's ragged shadows.
I am waiting for a birth
that will change everything: the earth
born over and over;
the cold eye of light slowly widening –
these hard buds guarding our unopened time.

★　★　★

Old Mother, give me of thy wood:
And I shall give some of mine
When I turn into a tree.

Candlemas

for my father, d. 2/2/81

On Brigid's Night
there was rain and wind and miles of darkness between us;
there was a generation of pain between us,
but I stayed awake for love's sake, and because of the candles.

On Brigid's Night
spring was calling a long way off, below the horizon
invisible, but heard, like a changed note;
my ears attuned, I lit candles around the room.

My children slept
upstairs, bundles of summer. I was tight-strung
and humming. Nineteen points of fire
in a small room needed watching: I sat with them.

My eyes half-closed
I watched them burn all night, watched wax spill pools
and curl and flow, the flames dip low,
wrapped round in shadows, caught in the eye of light.

The night you died
I talked to you through webs of sleep, recalling
you in my years of childhood
solid and sure, filling the fiery spaces.

I slept at last
towards dawn, in a darkened room. Slowly I woke
to sunlight striping the carpet, the cold
little heaps of wax: and my children shouting, and spring

one day nearer
and bottles clanking outside, and a sense of peace
and freedom; then the shrill cry
of the telephone, which I stumbled up to answer.

Wrinkles

The wrinkle words: their silent W
that is not quite silent, but waves to you
from the page, draws your mouth into an OO
without sound, that obsolete expletive.

All wrinkle words move, bend and twist:
I wring my hands so, with a turning wrist;
wretched I bow down, wrenching with my fist
at an old burden I can't get rid of.

I wrap a shawl around me; or my arms
around you. I wreak havoc, cause alarms:
bending and twisting, my huge wrath harms
and heals, shoots up, dies back and rankles.

I wrest this from your grasp; and we
wrangle, we wrestle, and you wriggle free:
we were both wrong; we turned perpetually
against the grain, we whirled in cross orbits.

Easy to wreck a world, to twist it out
of shape. With rapid skills we wrought
great wonders, turned our hands, but bent our thoughts
awry; we brought ruin, crooked changes.

As I write this, the words bend to and fro
like curling sea-wrack at the rim of a slow
wave: growing clouds beneath my window
writhe through the air. My thoughts are blown wraiths.

I watch the glass. I pull a wry face:
new wrinkles ruck and ripple, mark the place
where I've been wroth, or worried. I can trace
a wreath of smiles woven around my eyes.

Our crazy English spelling – those weird words
with odd unspoken letters and absurd
anachronisms! Here's an old-fashioned bird:
a wren. Her song, too, spirals, runs, and wrinkles.

The Gardener's Daughter

In the gloom of a dusty shed
       lay seed potatoes, rows of knobble faces
staring at me, exhaling a sharp reek
       of the underworld, stopping my breath with mould.
I'd sit with them, half-afraid,
       listening to the tinny noise of rain
and your voice from the outer world of the stone yard.

Your movements were large and slow,
       steady, skilful, lifting a laden barrow
with ease, in the long light of the afternoon;
       or in the sea-light of the glasshouses
you strung tomato trusses
       with their heavy, jungle smell,
and played the monsoon of the snaking hose.

My movements were quick and small
       making my feet ring on the iron floor,
following you along the leafy rows,
       plucking out weeds to please you.
Squat in my rubber boots I'd fill the pots
       shovelling compost with the narrow trowel,
proudly wearing my work in my fingernails.

I held the slipping knots
       as we wound raffia round squeaking stems
of tulips, freesias, dahlias: but you
       carried the precious flowers in your huge hands
much gentler than mine, to the water.
       And I, the gardener's daughter,
my face to the swimming blooms, conjuring rainbows.

The Trespasser

My fingers are sweet with stealing
blackcurrants. Among tall weeds
ropes of them, thick and ripe like secrets.
I move in shadow, sharp-eyed, listening.
A distant car sets my spine quivering.
Bold as a bird I pull the berries down,
gather them in. Their smell excites me.

The house is blind: no-one is living here,
yet I am trespassing. Each summer the owners
come for a week or two, cut grass,
clean windows, stare out from their gate.
Yet the river sings all year; and swifts make
nests, flowers bloom and fruit
ripens, and snow sweeps the lawn
smooth for the prints of foxes.

In spring there were daffodils, massed gold
and white narcissi; I ran in the rain
to gather armfuls, carrying them home
to shine in my windows. I live by here
every day, in poverty. What the hedges grow,
what's in the hills, I take back for my children.

Great polished blackcurrants in my fist.
They drop in the bag, grow fat.
Tonight I'll mix them with sugar and steam
them slowly. The dark, sour, smoky taste:
my children's red mouths and chins,
their high, bird voices. Each year the trees
step forwards round the house: I notice that.
In the autumn, I'll come for apples.

from Book of Shadows

To The Islands

Driving to Llanybydder from the hills
in sunlight, a clean blue sky
bathing us in its image: a light-pocket,
an open eye in all these weeks of rain,

we suddenly saw the sea in a strange place,
inland. We followed a new coast:
pale lucid water filled the low ground
to the west, and risen islands stood

netted with fields or thinly brushed
with trees; and shoreside cottages
whitewashed, perched over a harbour –
a landscape from the inner Hebrides

exact and stunning. Though of course we knew
it was only a trick of mist, sucked up
from unremarkable sodden earth, still
we cried out happily, "Look at the sea!"

So it shall be someday, when the polar ice
melts, and expanding oceans lift
over the land again. Sea licking
those hills into islands and promontories,

the Teifi swallowed into a sea-loch
and lush farms drowned, the hill farms turned
into fisherman's cottages. We could see
the future in a bowl of clear water,

seeing the present too, scrying the land
that is always there but mostly invisible –
the land's other face, the place where boats
put out from curved inlets, and green fields

tilt down to the sea; where eels thread
their way between tall hedges. Sun low
behind us, as far south as it will go,
as we ran into the outer blurs of mist

and the islands vanished. Above, we sensed
the summer colour of sky without seeing it:
and turning west, we crossed the plain grey river
in silence, like driving through water.

Feeding the Bat

At first it was a small cold palmful
a hunched and sorry scrap, clenched still
but for an infinitesimal buzz and tremble,

as we passed it from hand to hand
half fearful that the buzzing might explode
into uncontrollable flight. So we found

a box, and a place by the stove, and scrounged
a spoonful of dogfood from the corner shop
and waited. When the scratching started

we crowded round to listen: it was alive!
Lifting it out, it seemed larger; it moved
Its clever head from side to side, gave

delicate soundings. Two eyes, dark points of light
gleamed, not at all blind, and long questioning
fingers gripped mine. Whiskered like a cat,

with a cat's silken cunning it consented
to be fed from the end of a stick, opened
a triangle mouth wide, and dipped and lunged

manoeuvring meatlumps in. Laughing, we squeezed
waterdrops onto its nose, to hear it sneeze
minute bat-sneezes, to watch the supple greedy

slip of a tongue flick the droplets down.
As it warmed, it got bolder, nipping our skin
with needle teeth, unfolding its tucked wings,

turning its goblin face to the window, where
milky chilled spring daylight lured
it to sudden flight, skimming at head height

a strange slow flutter, followed by a whisper
of displaced air. Awaiting a change of weather
we hung it in a bag to sleep over the stairs

and roused it for feeding. After the second day
it arched its back to be stroked, and played
a biting game, neck stretched impossibly

backward, slyly grinning. That evening, the sun
shone. We carried it in its bag to a vacant barn
by the river. It squealed as I left it there, long

angry squeals; but I was firm. I would not
be quite a witch yet, stroking and feeding a bat,
my ears tuned to its music, swooping, flitting about –

though I lean out to the buoyant dusk, for all that.

Your Castle Picture

The sky comes right down to the ground
in your picture. And my eye's led
over scrawled ground to the castle,
solid and grey with its black slits,
its great dark ruined archways. You
have remembered a strange sight
of windows through the arch; they shine
deep blue in the crayoned shadows.

Tremendous – but is it right
that the sky should come down
all the way to the ground?
Last week, your sky was childish, high
and innocent, blue strip
at the top of the page, and white
air everywhere. I liked the way
the sun hung under it, with yellow
leggy rays. I liked the earth
swept safe beneath our feet. So
what's happened to bring the sky so low,
the earth so hunched and high?
The sun shrunk to a blurred smear
too bright to focus on?

I look at you, but your smile is clear colour,
glowing, unspoiled. There's a storm outside
blundering with charcoal clouds
I could almost paint. The sky
is close to us; it's scribbled on the ground.

Little son, as you ran shouting in the gale
I stuck your castle picture to my wall.

Moving the Boxes

(for Anabel)

This was the least I could give you:
My strength on the far side of a box
Packed with your hidden life, the weight
Of cheerful clutter, our years apart.
Our backs and arms were strong
Together, making a dance of it.

I pushed the sides shut, and you taped
All joins and edges tight against time
And weather; our eyes met over the stacks;
We laughed a lot. You folded summer clothes
For a distant season. It was work, tough
Labour, pressing the grief right down.

It was the last I could give you:
A catkin branch from the river, a clutch
Of snowdrops, their white winged faces;
My scrubbing-out of cupboards, scratch
Meals from the ends of packets, a spread
Of coloured cards: chances, changes.

And for me, the gathering-up of love
Giving me heart again. We could see
Each other now quite clearly without our men;
Our perfect, matched movements, our double power.
It was no trouble. The boxes are well-filled:
Now for the hard part. We'll share the load.

Brynberllan

(New Inn, Pencader)

This is a place where nothing really grows
but water; water and stones.

And concrete bungalows, and lost holdings.

Tilt of water from the mountainside
pushes under the road, and stones grow
overnight in our gardens: rainbuffed hard
perennials. We're on the flank
of the wind, even in summer.

But years ago, this was an apple orchard.

Rows and patterns of tress, all the way
down to the stream called *Comely*;
mossy-barked, their darkblue stems at dusk,
the sun spread white at dawn on slopes
of blossom; warm air, stirred thick
with honey. Humming, and swarms, and then
the smell of ripe fruit: those small
sharp western apples.

Crowded faces, bushels and basketfuls.

Everyone there, at work in the branches,
measuring the loads, brownarmed
and busy. Shouts in the crisp leaves.
Children rolling windfalls down the hill.
Foxes nosing at night through bruised grass.

And apple smoking in the soul-fires.

I think the traffic worsens year by year
just passing through. Rain's harsher too:
laced with acid and caesium, it fills
the stream called *Comely* and the stream
called *Blossom*. Nothing flourishes.

Yet sometimes we'll distil, between breath

and breath, a taste of sweetness:
yes, even now, a rustling of leaves,
a blossom-drift. Between low flakes
of October sunlight, treeshapes flicker:
and evenings to the West bring cloud-landscapes
rising like a range of wooded hills,
a place of apple-orchards. Not here: beyond

reach; elsewhere, forsaken, forfeited.

Llanthony Priory

It's a heathen rain today
driving over the high pass from Hay
falling in blown webs and torn shreds
over great weights and sacred elevations
raised to withstand the weathers of the world
now letting the wet world in;

falling on arches propping up the wind
falling on these stumps of sure foundation
falling in smoke-drift down the long nave
falling in a shaken benediction

over the damp chancel and shattered tower
over the drip, drip in the canons' kitchen
over the lost cloister and buried choir:

an irreligious rain. We stand in its lee
by a bit of stacked buttress.

Geese in a little paddock stuck with trees
stretch their rude necks at us. My children
yelling and running down the green slope
of the altar steps, chase round the sanctuary.
And in the prior's lodging, yellow elder
waggles her sexy fruits.

The ruins shape our gaze; they lift our eyes
to the hills, from whence cometh rain.
The immanent and omnipresent hills
which were always there, during Lauds and Vespers,
a mighty unseen eminence, like God
waiting beyond the walls. And now
they've broken through that careful masonry
in a pantheon, tremendously circled,
splendidly photogenic, framed in stone.

I lift my camera, and wander round
to capture an alignment. Dewi's rain
gusts down from Wales, floating in fine drops

in your mossy hair. Our Lady pours
dark red in rivers from the mountainside
chanting perpetual sorrows. Holy wells
are rising. Litanies and psalms
from vivid, potent, scarlet tongues of bracken.

These sharpedged, lovely lines
are spare and windswept, leave us comfortless.
You huddle in your coat. Let's go back soon,
and sample the real ale at the Half Moon.

A Northwest Passage

(An autopsy on the frozen bodies of three of the members of Franklin's last expedition revealed that they died of lead poisoning from contaminated tinned food.)

Franklin's seaman lies in a dream of ice:
his brain's turned into an oval lump
of solid ice. It fills
his skull with a cloudy whiteness.

His body is unchanging, six feet
down in the permafrost. He has forgotten
sunlight through green leaves,
tartness of orchard apples, the warm
loam of Kent. In his cells
an Arctic silence. His last thoughts frozen.

What made them sew him up
warmly in all his shirts? Was it
to keep him from the cold?
Why did they struggle with clumsy picks
ringing on frozen gravel, hour after hour
in shrieking winter darkness
chipping and spitting ice, to make graves?

Was it love, in that awful place?

This decent, graceful gift:
A red cloth laid like a prayer
over his face, hiding the terrible clamp

of pain, the lips drawn back
over uneven teeth, the eyes locked.
Too tall for the hasty coffin, they crammed him in
with one arm twisted beneath him.

John Torrington, John Hartnell, William Braine:
abandoned with their chiselled names
in a dead time, poison in their bones,
their guts, their hair. In Arctic time

the wind is a true presence:
the sky is the world
surrounding a small circle of shifting ice.

And the names of the trapped ships
Terror and *Erebus*
are a dreadful presence; and the names
of Franklin and his crew
dragging the weight of a slow death
blindly over the snow, daft wanderers
searching for a way through,

stumbling into the sun, are a presence.

The Sealwife

One day I shall find my skin again:
my own salt skin, folded dark, its fishweed stink
and tang, its thick warm fat, great thrusting tail

all mine; and I'll take it and shake it out
to the wind, draw it over me cool and snug,
laugh softly and slip back to my element.

I shall find my stolen skin, hidden by you
for love (you said) that night the sea-people danced,
stashed in some cleft in the rocks where I may not go

but used to go, and dance too, stepping free
in my new peeled body, the stalks of my legs in the moon-
light strange, my long arms shaping the sky

that have narrowed their circles down
to the tasks of these forked hands: lifting,
fetching, stirring, scrubbing, embracing –

the small, stiff, landlocked movements. In the sea
I plunged and swam for my own joy, sleek and oiled,
and I loved at will in rolling-belly tides.

Here love is trapped inside the walls of a house
and in your voice and eyes, our children's cries;
whose boundaries I've understood, a language

learnt slowly, word by word. You've been dear and good –
how you would sing to me, those wild nights! –
and oil my breasts by firelight, and dip down

to taste my sea-fluids. I'd forget to mourn
those others then, trawling the flickering deeps.
Now I cry for no reason, and dream of seals:

an ocean booms in the far cave of my ear,
and voices tug at me as I stand here
at the window, listening. Our children sleep

and by daylight they run from me. Their legs
strong, their backs straight, bodies at ease
on solid ground – though they play for hours on the shore

between sand and sea, and scramble the wet rocks
gladly. It won't be long now, the waiting –
they love to poke and forage in the cracks

of the cliffs; sharpeyed, calling, waving.

The Bee-flight

(Bredwardine, Herefordshire)

That was a strange, rare place, in a loop
between river and nippled hill
with a crooked sandstone church and trees
that corkscrewed, and a massive leaning yew
one thousand years thick, peeled rosy flesh,
and a woman carved into the north wall
with legs agape, and a man with a bird's head
whistling sorcery. The ground rose
in hummocks: the past, carelessly buried,
trying to break through. Snowdrops showed white
and wet below the mound. I stood at the cusp
of spring in a frayed landscape
bleached-out by frost, stripped clean

as an old bone, sucked dry. I'd thought
there was nothing to fill me, nothing to speak to me;
but here was rain smelling of turned earth,
the sun in watercolour, curved paths,
storybook trees, bark swirled, bulged-out and fissured
peopling the place. At the edge of a pool
a straddled oak with a hole
at eye level, forced me to stare. Birds calling, then
a humming past my ear, and again: brown bees
sailing in from the sedges, dipping down
into darkness, hollow mouth-oak, in and in
with grains of new gold. A ragged shower blew
up from the west. Something unfolding, stirring

under my feet. The lumpy, breast-topped crag
now spiralled in light; the birdman suddenly answered
by choruses of wings, and the opened thighs
of the sandstone witch by the presence of flying bees.

Breakfast with the Poets

(Almería, Andalusia)

Dawn at the Alcazaba.
The poets come
up from the drowsy city, appearing like birds
from a woven nest of alleys;
some walking, most in cars
turning difficult corners in the dark,
all drawn to the honey rock

in scores, in hundreds
from under stones, from a breeze in the desert,
the folds of the sea. They've come
with spouses, friends and children, greeting
each other on the steps of the citadel
of light. That woman in evening dress
hasn't slept all night. That child,
like ours, stares through us,
eyes blank with dreams. They climb
and we climb with them
through the sultan's exquisite garden
shaping word after word.

Up in the high courtyard
are men with microphones, women
trailing long veils. Everyone laughs, delighted.
We lean together over rose-coloured walls
and watch the sun
rise over stripped hills, ruined terraces.
This is a strange country
breeding poets instead of flies. They swarm
in the pure, steady light.

They hand out dazzling blankets:
like loaves and fishes, it's a miracle:
everyone sits down. Music swells
in a wild, muezzin cry.
A woman lifts brown arms, releasing
a pigeon. *See, I have laid*

my greeting in the collar of a dove
which will fly over the land
of Almería like a flung censer.

The poets read in turn,
women and men, intensely,
darkly and gloriously. Children wriggle.
I can't understand
all the words either; but they seem
poems of celebration.

Morning expands and blazes: the sun hits
the wall above us with a gold fist.
The city is awake: it roars
and glitters in the wilderness; *a bucket*
of whitewash thrown at the mountains.
Comrade poets, ladies, gentlemen:
now breakfast will be served;
herb tea and spicecakes in the high tower
of Ibn Al-Mu'tasim.

from the sequence Book of Shadows

I Book of Shadows

Behold now, before you, the man who has pierced the air and penetrated the sky,
journeyed among the stars and soared beyond the margins of the world....
Giordano Bruno, La Cena dei Ceneri

Under the shadow of the good and true
I am feeling, groping my way through an inner room
a mole in a mass of roots, no a fish among weeds
seeing and touching in silence by greenshift sun.
Holding it all, holding it all together:
gathering-up, mending the smashed mirror –
seven thousand years' bad luck – and here's the one
clear perfect image, the crazed world newly reflected,
turning in unison, its scattered notes
tumbling into a song: building, joining-up
atom to atom in the universe
in a great golden chain. The bee flies out

from its close monastic cell, never having seen
flowers, but having an image of flowers
somewhere imprinted, sees and smells and knows
the source of sweetness, burrowing with joy
and bringing treasure home. I am a bee.
The different colours of flowers do not confuse me.

So I make, comb by comb, my magic book –
my Book of Shadows. Its pages flicker and gleam
as if seen underwater; its letters red and black,
its curious diagrams, mad conjurations
scud in and out of light, unreadable.
But as I draw it slowly from the pool
of Imagination, look! It becomes plain, easy.
This is magic: what I do. I have come to you
with the world up my sleeve and heaven in my hat
shuffling a clutch of pictures. On my pied robe
I've sewn the stars invisible: they are inside,
within, where they should be – Luna and Sol,
Mercury, Bootes, the Bull, the Banquet.

Now shut your eyes. I can make you see them too:
stars in a meadow, knuckles on a tree,
galaxy shells, lost cities at low tide
shouldering out of the slime. Hold it all, all
precious and rare, mind-mirror, dazzling round
Book of infinite pages, colours, shadows and sound.

II Athene

Her have I loved and sought from my youth, and desired for my spouse,
and have become a lover of her form…and I prayed…that she might be
sent to abide with me, that I might know what I lacked…for she knew and
understood… G. Bruno: Oratio Valedictoria

First, they made me an eye.
In the cold revolving stars, in the storm,
in the flying sun, in the place where water
comes out of the earth, an eye.
The eye watched: they were not alone.
They scratched its shape on stones
where the dead lay. Its rays spun out
weblike, encompassing the world;
drilled into bone, a passage, a way through.

Next, they made me a brow.
Over two staring circles, a double bow,
thick plunging curves, a look
of intense concentration. Life
with some thought behind it, an intelligence.
By now, they'd invented pots:
comfortable pregnant bellies, with twin eyes
frowning out of the clay. Sense
out of nonsense: room to grow.

Then came the owl: that was natural.
Something alive and searching after dark –
that great dished listening face.
Soundless flight; wings a whisper of snow,
then the sudden swoop of death.
The voice of a world both fearful and beautiful
Was a shuddering *hoo,hoo.* That suited me.

I flew secretly; I stunned, I wooed,
I tore apart, I saw and heard all.

And lastly, a woman born
out of sea-foam, out of flowers, or from
the head of a god – ridiculous. I'd been
too generous: the people thought too much;
they gorged on metaphors, they killed for them.
I was Athene, wise and terrible,
flinging my spears, helmeted with the Moon,
crowned with stars, a woman clothed with the Sun
defending Right and Might and Truth and Freedom.

But now, little monk, by dusk
I see you kneeling on the cold flags
of your narrow cell, and your mind
is all eyes. In your heart a dark fire,
a lust. You have trusted me
and I have come; but I will not come kind
or maidenly – never forget, I am taloned,
banished from daylight, savage with desire –
but beautiful, yes my love; and I see, I see.

III The Inner Artificer

Man labours on the surface of things; but Nature works from within.
G. Bruno: De Causa

The scientist's posed in a pigsty –
an awkward smile on his round foolish face –
with his creature, transgenic monster, poor pig,
blind, bloated, and arthritic, a coarse slab.
That smile of hesitant triumph,
those well-scrubbed fingers touching the prone
thick body in the straw, show no remorse,
more a coy, teasing promise, an allure.

And I wonder, Bruno, what you'd think of him
that gene-magician in his white coat,
his surface-work. They still say *Mother Nature* –
meaning a woman, weak and pliable,

limited, passive, open to be explored,
discarded, raped. Mother gives more and more.

But among us, *da noi*, Nature is called
the inner artificer. And she's everywhere,
strong, steadfast; power in the womb
of matter, the spirit that shines
through things. She's a voice
heard in a room, sounding to each corner,
everywhere resonant: we can't turn from her.

And she returns us our filth, feeds us
our stored-up poison. She will not spare
the seals, or our children. Deserts balloon,
malignant. As we divide, negate,
reduce and separate, she multiplies,
joins and reshapes the world, swarms out
from the core. She is not sentimental.

This grinning alchemist plays with the parts,
blind to the whole. Like his pig
he is paralysed, stuck, sterile. He believes
in the old, flat, static earth: he believes in Hell.

While Nature still works from her centre,
expelling galaxies, singing through every door.
Revolutionary Queen of the chromosomes,
the inner artificer. Hidden and sure.

X The Revolving Castle

The Infinite Universe moves in circles…like the turning of a wheel; which remains
motionless in itself, while all its parts are turning. – G. Bruno: Eroici Furori

The small spiders of spring weave webs of spun droplets
catching newly-hatched light in their filaments,
veiling their world in gauze, through which they regard
our world of crystal. Each sound, each touch
is magnified. Spiders wear their nerves
outside, in the air, their thoughts running along
the gummy, plucked strands like music.

Dark thoughts: dark, rapid music.
The trees, stone walls, wet crumbling banks, are hung
with spider-minds, revolving spiral visions
strummed in the wind. Perhaps this early sun
will bring them careless midges. The spring spiders
wait quietly for luck, one fine leg poised
to feel its tug. When it comes, it will be sudden.

> I too: I have been spinning.
> I've spread my mind out
> in coils of silk, joining
> stone to star, word to tree.
> I peer through its threads
> at all worlds, the circles
> expanding, drawing in.
> It seems there are doors
> between them, mostly hidden.

What have I started? What have I set in motion?
These wheels – where will they take me? Something
is bound to happen, some shaking of the web.
I wrote my desire in wax, and transmuted it
to flame. I'm not like you, Giordano:
I'm afraid, and careful; more pliable, less fixed,
not honed to your brilliant point. You are all
swords; I'm spiderlike, labouring
in the dark, through touch, web-maker,
a bowl of water. *Spring is coming, not long now* –
and then, Summer. All our spells return on us.
Turning woman, spinning woman am I...
I can fly as high as you, for all your boasting,
and fall as hard, and make magic as lasting.

XIV Alchemy

We are in a state of continual transformation: fresh atoms are continually being incorporated in us, while others that we received beforehand escape from us .– G. Bruno: De l'Infinito

Wonderful what will come out of darkness:
stars, owl voices, sleep;

water, green shoots, birds' eggs
with their own curved darkness;

gemstones; a whole and perfect child
from my unseen recesses; delight

from behind shut lids, finding each other,
fingers and tongues made magical by night.

Great magic's performed after sunset.
Old alchemists conjuring angels,

witches dancing spirals under the moon;
drum-shamans, their spirit journeys;

two nights in a tomb
before a resurrection. Transformations

taking place out of ordinary sight.

Daylight gives us boundaries, fixes
everything. The world separates

into colours and chemicals, figures
and faces. Surfaces appear solid,

reliable, unconfused. We can see
to operate complex machinery.

Only darkness permits mixing
of elements, stirring of essences

in secret, combing dark and bright
into new patterns while we sleep; so dawn

finds us transformed, shifted. Star
particles link us with trees,

dolphins and stones, travel through us,
creating the universe. Base matter

becomes gold: in the Cauldron
of Annwn, in the crucible of mind

we're all magicians. The Hidden Stone,
Elixir of Life, eludes us; we've lost

the art of working through touch
with invisible forces; but as darkness

rises, and we grope wildly
for other hands to hold, out of dissolution

and chaos perhaps the magic will come right.

XVIII The Voyager

The soul is not in the body: the body is in the soul. It is steeped in the soul as a net in the sea.

Wisdom is set in our spirit, seated on the poop of our soul, holding the tiller of the ship which it steers across the tempestuous seas of the century. – G. Bruno: Gli Eroici Furori ; Oratio Valedictoria

I'm your silver, I'm your guide in the night, your dancer,
your voyager sailing the storm, your adventurer
feathered strokes dipping waterskin, a rainbow dazzle
flung out on the tips of my wings, the whisperer
in your inner ear, your deceiver, impossible sweet
changing-faced lover, your infinitely wild
passionate unrestrained your divine possessor,
who rises and shines above time and reflects
the universe in your mind, the torch that shows
all your coloured images; I'm a dolphin-rider
dragging you into the sea, strange shapes in the water
rising to meet, dissolving you bone from bone, a
bitter solution, drinking you in; I'm your muse
I'm your madness, your loneliness, wanting you only
for me to play my rays on, be mirrored in your eyes,
surprise and creep up behind, to find you out,
turn you round about and devour you, feed you
to the wolves, chop and change you, rearrange
your careful thoughts, circles of memory unspun

flung overboard and drowned; but plunge deep
in me, they'll be found whole and new, restored
if you trust me: I'm your last hope, your saviour
healer and teacher, your light when all lights
go out, your mariner. So follow me, take my hand;
let me sidle into your dreams, there's no need to be
afraid, I'm only the shadow, pure moonlight, look
through me and see the sun rise, the voyage made.

from ANIMACULTURE

Animaculture

The gardening angels tuck their robes
into their belts, pull their boots on,
cover their heads with haloes and set out

to cultivate the world. Each one
has hoe and sickle, spade and watering-can
and wings, and a small patch

to care for. They come in all colours:
dawn, rain or dusk, rose, marigold,
moss, midnight; gliding between

reflections, rarely seen. At three
years old, occasionally I'd catch
the flick of a wing, a glitter on the air

a tickle of warmth behind me, someone there
playing roll-in-the-grass with me
pushing my swing. And at night

my gardening angel laid her head
beside me, smelling of daisies,
and breathed with me. At my maiden flight

along our street, my feet grazing the privet,
past lamp-posts and garden gates, her voice
in my ear steered me and said –

This is the way to Heaven, along here.
Since then, so many false choices:
knotted with weeds, I'm overgrown

and parched as dust. Who will open
the door to the garden, who will water
me now? Wise child, I trusted my own

right words, I knew the angel's name,
and that death was part of the game.
I find it very hard to remember her.

The gardening angels prune and propogate
moving in secret through the soul's acres —
have I called on mine too late?

Whistling, she strolls in from long ago,
And she hands me the rake and hoe —
Your turn, she says; and I feel my wings stir.

Making Babies

The child gives her mother a drawing of Heaven.
A blank place, empty of trees
and sun, and houses; just that
lumpy cloud mattress underfoot and angels
shuffling through the cirrus
with wings askew, with haloes
balanced over their heads like upturned "O"s,
like jugglers' plates at the end of their spin.
One teeters nervously, struck rigid
on round feet studded with toes.

But this is God's show, and He upstages
all others. The child imagines Him
darkbearded, genial, whistling while He works.
She explains this to her mother, who sews
cross-stitches in pink and blue silks
on a dollsized creamy smock, who threads
a smile all ready, her needle poised
before she's even looked. *There's God*
the child informs her, *making babies.*
In fact it seems He could be moving house:

surrounded by boxes labelled BLOOD, BONES,
HAIR, SKIN, and so on. Here are His raw
materials: the Blood Box brims.
She's drawn Him at the instant of His power,
a conjuror with something up
those bulky sleeves, to flourish
with a flash and pop! – then paeans of applause
from the stunned, golden hosts.
Her mother laughs. *You funny little girl!*
The child frowns, flushed. he knows

what's tucked beneath her mother's print
frock, what grows there; she understands
what blood is, and skin, and hair,
the speech of her heart on her pillow – but can't
translate it. How should she draw
the fat, packed world? – vivid as sleight-of-hand,

clumsy as that play about angels,
improbable as death or dinosaurs
or Heaven buzzing like a swarm of dreams,
out there where anything goes.

Ursa

for Robert Minhinnick

Sleep makes you hungry. I could eat stones, leaves,
beetles, birch bark. These are my woods:
I recognise the tangle and muddy hollows, quick
rustle, the sun threading down like this.

I tread in warm slabs of sun. I flounder
to my knees in snow clumps, blue in the shade.
Winter shrinks back. My heart's dull step
has kicked into a run. My slack lungs swell,
unfurl like rubber wings. I'm awake now.

Look at me: I am bigger than before.
My body shakes with each stride. I lower
my head to the torrent, swallow green thaw,
let it cool my fire. I eat. Blood in my mouth,
sweet salmon flesh. Still I need more than this.

Through the dark time, I huddled in a hole
with my arms over my face, my blood slurred
thick in my veins, my tongue stuffed like a gag
in my throat. Sometimes my soul would claw
its way out and climb the great spruce
arm over arm toward the arclight

of the moon, and all the forest
hushed in frost. Or else on days of storm
it blundered from tree to tree, torn by the gale
into rags, flew about roaring. Blizzard. The din
of branches, like hunters closing in.

But I'm alive again. I am solid, wrapped round
in sleek black hide. My claws and teeth gleam.
You saw me shuffle up from the trout stream, turning
stones over, questioning the ground. I ignored you: my mind
is on something better, my mind is on treasure.

Something found only by digging; a glow in the dirt,
in the forest floor. Under rocks, under roots, what my heart
needs, what my soul feeds on. I will turn every stone
on earth, until I find what I'm looking for.

Drawing Down the Moon

for Tim Rossiter

First, clear a space for it.
The moon needs room to breathe,
to swell and shrink.
And don't just think of the white disc,
but the light around it.

Remove all rocks and stumps,
nettles and cabbages. Be
ruthless: this snare must be smooth
as a coin, and fine
as the skin of your eye.

Next, take a rope, and cast
your circle. May everything
in the ring attract moonshine.
Then hammer wooden pegs
around the shape, pulled hard

against the wind, which would carry
your garden, moon and all,
away, if it could. Remove
your coat, and get digging.
Right down to the subsoil,

two foot deep in the middle,
shelving towards one end. Use
a level: if the ground tilts
your prize will spill. Heap the spoil
high to the south, for shelter.

Strew sand for a bed
and tread it firm. Ignore
your neighbours' sidelong glances
as you unroll stout polythene
to keep the precious rays

from running out.
Stretch it tight across the hole,

weigh it down with stones
and feed in liquid
to the brim. Stand back

in admiration. Wait
until nightfall. Say
the spell: and behold the moon
in your garden, swimming up
through nets of water.

Behind the Waterfall

The waterfall is at its best today:
properly huge, it booms from its rock wall
in a curve of white sound –
an upturned river, fat with rain,
dense with crushed water, a sideways pull
that draws the whole world.
Up close, you can feel a wet gale
sucking you in, tugging at the trees
whose branches dance away

and my children clamber and call.
I don't worry, they're big now, this is their
place, behind the waterfall,
while motherly I stand here
on solid rock, to be someone to wave at,
to witness their daring.
Their voices are lost in the clamour
of fractured water, of foam
fragments that change form slowly
as they fall, stretching like gum
in emptiness before smashing, reforming

running away. Through a mask of spray
I see them waving:
grey boy and lilac girl
fading and blurred, aslant
behind the torrent, unfocussed
billion tiny lenses dropping through time
and space, holding this moving shape
together, this strange attractor
through which we grin and gesture.

When my son suddenly hugged me yesterday
he had to stoop – a year ago
I stooped to hug him – and he felt light and cool
as rain on my cheek; then out
of my arms and up to his full height
still growing. And my daughter

though she runs like a child, under her lilac sweater
the shadow of breasts in this light.

The waterfall roars between them and me.
Fluid, unbreakable, a closed gate
of running glass through which
they waver and stand
beyond reach yet visible, mouthing
excitedly, deafened by the sound
of waterforms changing, exploding
escaping, unstoppable, sweeping us all
before it, downstream. And when
they return, shaking the thunder from their brains,
soaked through and laughing, it's like meeting
again, after a journey, after a dream.

Dandelions

My yard's unweeded, warm with dandelions
I will not cut away till they whiten;
honey-scented rays on worn stone
blazing bravely. Banished from the rich
green sterile fields, they crowd
the roadside like beggars, they loiter,
turning on passers-by their gold eyes.
Milk from their snapped stems stains dark
and bitter, they are no respecters of persons,
their leaves ragged and toothed, crude pissabeds,
long rooted, fecund, shameless. Yellow
gypsies, raggle taggle, camped
at the margins, the city plots,
waste lots and motorway verges:
largely ignored, driven out, returning.

Today I have sat with them
tearing yellow from green, yellow from green
for four hours, my fingers sore and brown,
for wine thin and sharp as a cat's stare
with a heart that burns small, gleaming
honeycomb heart. My daughter brings
a handful, bunched like suns
in her round fists. She squats hard
on her heels, black gypsy eyes
narrowing in the light. She smiles,
and blows a seedhead, counting.

Star-gossamers float, touch
down invisibly on next-door's lawn,
needle between the blades, stitch themselves in.

Mother Anthony's

(Mother Anthony's Well, in Mother Anthony's Wood, nr. Devizes, Wiltshire)

Looking for the well in the wood,
the named well in the named wood,
looking for a source, a spell
of water from rock, from soil
from the veins of trees –
and never quite finding it

we visited, we revisited
in all seasons, with the wood blown
and bare, or sappy and plush
full of voices, to discover
a stream without source, whose source
shifted from rock to swamp
to cornfield. What we found

wasn't the named well, but something
unnameable. A tingle beneath skin.
The way all paths led downwards,
crouched under boughs. And the stream
stone cold, with a crushed taste.

Once there were hares racing
at dusk up and down the hill
as we approached, oblivious to us.
Once a thunderstorm
that pelted us from the trees
into the parched stubble of the fields.

We visited, we revisited.
We found a bottle buried in a pool,
old bubbled glass. Sometimes
we'll drink from it, toast Mother Anthony,
looking for what was lost.

What Brynach Saw

(Carn Ingli, Pembrokeshire)

Someone saw angels on this hill.
One of those early saints, the tough
weathered sort with big hands
and knotty calf-muscles; the wild-eyed
sort gazing into a grey gale,
cloak bucking round him; rough
jawed and broken-toothed from an old brawl
those nights before he fell in love
with the sky and became a saint.

A youth spent handling cattle,
hacking at stumps, cutting peat in the rain
to stack in low skewed rows
for the wind to dry. Planting beans, stooped
to earth; wrestling a boar down
for gelding in the swamp of the yard –
the screams, the stink, the swearing.
Brynach. A lad with a dusk thirst
no cask of ale could kill.

Parched, he longed to drink light
in bellyfuls, to feel clouds
surge through him. Watched swifts
dart and skim, watched the kite
hover. Fledged in the new religion,
discovered heaven as the mountaintops
sliced into his mind: dark blades
of ice, slipped scree. Here he stepped free
from flesh, from that long battle.

Alone with his love, arms out
to the sun like a heathen, he felt
the wind lift and hold him aloft
like the breath of God. From this height
the world is beautiful. You can carry it

all in your hands, the little stonewalled fields,
the sea leaping. You can see
what Brynach saw: how angels in the hill
raise their stone wings for flight.

from Sculpture at Margam

Miranda Brings the Sea to Margam

(Miranda Whall, resident sculptor, Margam Park Port Talbot, Oct-Dec 1992)

First of all, she cycled to the sea,
drawing a fine thread
from the copper trees;
under the motorway with a whisper
of spokes, a cobweb glitter

through the steelworks' grey
indifference, riding into
the molten sun, weaving a way
between hedgebanks to the shore.
Broad, empty sand; hammered water

curled towards her. She hooked
a scarf of surf and drew it up
tight; she spooled and locked
the sea-wind round her wrist
pulling it after, wound in her fist.

Back at the park, she propped
the bike, untangling
herself. Each holt and coppice
shone; but now, beneath the leaves
there's a tang of salt: the sea breathes.

★

Felt: the first fabric
from the age of ice.

Ice scoured these hills,
lay like soap in the valleys

while women pounded wool
with grease and snow-melt

making hats and shoes,
folding their babes in felt.

The dead swaddled too,
under the ice, sleeping.

Miranda, surrounded by bundles
of combed wool, is making

felt to dip in the sea.
It smells of washday

as she scoops a soap solution
through an old net curtain

till the wool's sodden,
dissolves its oils, knits fast.

She wraps the sandwich round a wooden pole
cross-gartered with a stocking
squeezes, then unpeels the nets
and carries the sheets to the shore.

One by one, she spreads them to the tide:
dog-walkers, joggers pass all afternoon

as she hauls her salt catch in
and seasons it with copper, sea-green.

Now she has rolled the sea
like a carpet, and stacked it here

it small felt coils and cones
snug for the winter, as ice crinkles

the air, and the last leaves drop.

★

This is a work of time
she says.

The Park is a clock
counting the hours

the tide-clock, the slow
pendulum of the sea.

The beeches have dropped their gold:
the flesh beneath blooms
with verdigris.
These new bright copper cones
will grow sea-green,
their pink cut wounds
healed over:

and the road-scar
and the city of oil and flame
will fade, and a skin of trees
will knit together

given time, and weather.

§

A Week Away

for Carol Ann Duffy

Falling asleep behind the folded door
I felt my grandmother lean into her chair:

I heard her needles flicker
through wool, the click of her cup

in its saucer, and I pictured
the blue veins purling her hands;

lulled by the warp and creak of the caravan,
the soft roar of the stove, the squeal

from her kettle, a whisper
of gaslight, the creamy sheet by my mouth.

But every night I dreamed of my own house
ablaze, burnt to a husk, crushed

by earthquake or explosion, cleft
with lightning like a tree

or filled with the thick green water
of the lake, and my parents drowned.

And once I found the rooms furnished with echoes –
they'd gone, and I was left.

Waking with snared breath and my face
wet, in a burrow of bedclothes

as my grandmother's footsteps moved
between supple walls, I'd lie

screened-off, a girl in a box, slotted
in place, and I'd listen to rain

drum on the tin roof, and hear
the slosh and clank of the enamel can

at the sink, and think of my family
shrunken by distance into blurred dots

that swam away from me. If I ever
saw them again, they'd be strange

and they'd smell of elsewhere; their eyes
would stare past me at another child

a little behind my shoulder.
And I'd find my clothes grown suddenly

tight, and myself much older.
Sometimes not even stone is strong enough:

when the people leave, the roof sags,
the windows crack, the house falls.

I used to feel I held the house aloft
somehow, by living in it.

This week, listening to the thin rain
breaking on someone else's tiles, I think

I've been away from home too long –
I shall return to find the house dwindled,

my hair brushing the ceiling, my elbows
jarring the walls, and everyone gone.

Deep Song

At school, we all sang soprano
sending our voices clear
through the tops of our heads,

our new-bloom women's bodies
ethereal beneath the stiff
pleated maroon,

and as the notes flew up, we rose too,
hovering on plumes of pure sound,
the shriven vowels of nuns.

But between puppyfat and agelines
I lost that voice, I lost
all angelic strivings,

visible now out of that uniform
of fluting descants, visible
and fleshly, having descended

to earth, my substance.
Now when I sing my voice rises
not from my throat, but lower,

from my centre, from the ground.
I've found my true voice in the register
of trees and stones and water:

so growing up means growing down
and deeper in. I've left heaven
to the birds with their child voices

while I rework the element of earth,
stir it with blood, with an old
unholy laughter. Listen:

the held note of the earth;
its pitched drone keys
all my music. This is my sphere:

its voice my voice.
I only visit the air
in rare dreams of a childhood spent there.

from Spring in Saskatchewan
for Jeanne-Marie de Moissac, and others

Water

Here they're called sloughs, pronounced *slews*:
springfed pools in the vast dry dome of the prairie.

Water that stands alone, watching the sky,
that makes a print of the sky; a film

moving over its lens, with clouds
blowing out and upward, miles deep.

The earth opens, revealing the stratosphere,
the wind, the thinning air. Your face a shadow

featureless, as you lean against the light
to look in. we are blanked out by height

and depth and distance, silhouettes, little dancing sticks
on the broad flank of the world. The slough's

view: eyeless heads and peeled limbs,
a brief disturbance of vision. The white blur

of ice is gone, snow blindness. This is spring:
reed-tips prickle its skin. Its feathers ruffle.

Ducks settle over its heart. Its water-body
contains the whole sky. Out here at dusk

you can watch darkness seep along the land,
spread over the sky like paint; you can feel

the tilt of the earth, the roll away from the sun.
a great beast turning over. The sloughs its eyes.

This one, teeming with frogs, a cacophony
of sex and ecstasy, full moon frog rave.

The grit road a pale smear, rubbed out
by coming footsteps of night. Winter is over.

The land breathes, water sees, birds meet
and couple, frogs party, sky soars, the horizon uncurls.

Soon green will spike the dun stalks. Crocus glances blue
through sagebrush. Sweetgrass. This is the eye of the world.

Fire

She walks out onto the deck
Her washing basket heavily cradled
To meet the sun newly ablaze this morning
The sky flying a blue sheet over the prairie

We step down into her garden
What passes for a lawn is still hummocked with winter
The action of frost, but here are green blades
Appearing like thoughts of summer

The day shivers with the promise of heat

She hauls her basket over to the line
Today she will pin the clothes outside
Show them to the sun

Children's tights with woolly nubbles of wear
Husband's denims dense and weighty as boards
Cotton checked shirts with frayed cuffs
Underwear discoloured from months of washing
Battalions of socks

Side by side we peg them to the breeze
Coldweather clothes, suddenly out of season

How intimately I am touching their lives!
Her little boy's pyjamas, her daughter's slip
Her husband's shorts, the small sewn towels she uses
Faintly shadowed with blood

And now the telling of secrets, shaking them out
On the warm grass under the washline

*

Afterwards she takes me to the pasture
We peel away our layers and lie down

The sun pours honey-balm
We are pale and cool, invisibly burning

The washing is dry by lunchtime

Strange how you can burn without knowing
In the bare spring sun
So it's only when evening falls your skin flames

How summer comes in a day

from GREENLAND

Ode to Rain

Rain you are everywhere
filling the air with glassy molecules
and the slow hiss of your outbreath as you glide

pulling the sky around you like a hood
and wiping the horizon
to a chalky smell:

you hit the ground running and scoot along
till you find a way in
going under to where you gather

for another ride through wood and leaf.
You are blood of the earth and river food
and ocean seed, mud maker

mountain shaper, carver of rock and cliff
stone polisher, road shaker –
yet so thin-skinned you shatter at a touch:

each water-bead breaking over the hills
and rooftops, cracking open
like soft eggs spilling dew.

Rain you climb in from the sea
laden with sea-sweat and the siphoning
of forests, falling in multitudes

jostling and whispering all night
a water-engine vibrating, a water flute
pitched to a low note, a gutter murmur.

So I wonder, what are your plans for us?
Will you trample us like grass and wheatstalks
and bend our heads down like the heads of roses

or soften us like fruit and cover us
with a bloom of rot? Will you wash us clear
of all dirt and colour, edges blurred together

with trees, towers, bridges, houses
one liquid grey dissolving
like paint left out in the weather?

Rain you have shut your dark doors
you have drawn your curtains around us
you have made our days fluid and porous

we see the world through your lens
shrunk to a dot at the end of a cloud funnel —
a dim flicker of light like a fishes' tail.

Soon we shall have to learn to breathe water
and stand like trees drinking rain
catching it in our outstretched palms

or else grow fins like every other creature
and swim the drowned streets to the river
spreading over the land and ending up somewhere

unrecognisable. If this is your purpose
too bad: we'll grumble as we've always done;
but though you beat on our tiles till they're worn

to shell-transparency we'll gaze through them
at any gap in the clouds, and see there
the first footprint of the sun.

Making Landfall

One morning you wake to a difference
in the touch of the air:
somewhere a door is open

the smell of the world comes in
and flutters round you
as if stirred by wings

as if borne your way on a shore wind
to the deck of your narrow ship
after months at sea –

an imprint of what waits below the horizon
beyond the grey expanse
cold heave of water

to reach you now, coffee and motor oil
fresh flowers and new-baked soil
warm rub of concrete

an onrush of green, an invasion
of leaves and spices:
a tang of sweat follows

and the world arrives and immediately begins
to reassemble its forms
out there on the edge of sight

On such a morning you notice the birds –
the shapes their bodies make
in free flight

Flock

There they go, slicing across my window
milliseconds before the rush of wings
whose echoes sweep the glass

banking as they pass
over rooftops, quartering the gardens,
the street grid, the back lanes.

Caught in the searchlight
of the sun against a sky of slate
now they are changed to steel,
to airfix models painted and glued together

flown synchronous and smooth
as if pulled sideways by an invisible hand –

the drill and hum of feathers all vibrating
in unison, the drumroll of their hearts.

Somewhere a pigeon keeper
waits on them

releases them each morning
to dart into the day with a clap of plumes,
rising over the terrace
wheeling above the park

like a handful of coins tossed
skyward by a lottery millionaire.

He is the backyard warden who holds the keys
to unlock the trick of flight,
who welcomes them to the home made loft at night

who measures every grain,
scours their clotted lime

cradles each quilled body in his palms
to check the swell of its crop
and gazes into the circle of each eye

fingers each scaly leg with clip and ring,
names them, calls them his loves,
his nest of doves

and presses his ear to the coop
at midnight, drawn to the murmuring
within, the downy shuffle

in the odorous dark.

Out With My Broomstick

I'm out with my broomstick in the pearly light
between dark and day
between sleep and waking
the streets like ancient rivers
lie open to the sky

I glide on my scuffed pole with its tatty broom-end
sparse and no good for sweeping but still it flies
a hands breadth over the pavement
trailing its battered furze

the stick itself is long and extends behind me
ready for the children to clamber on
the children I've come to ferry through the air
perched in my wake like ducklings

and here's a clutch of them gathered by a gateway
jostling like leaves

if a breeze sprang up they'd scatter across the road
but they turn their faces towards me
in simple trust and expectation of magic
that it may fall like a cloak protecting them
from winds both low and high

so they embark one by one
making the pole dip like a divining rod
but we clear the ground and just skim over the privet
startling passers-by
we are held in the air by a wisp
a sliver of thought

and now I've delivered my charges my task is done
    I'm free to fly my own way
    I mount the broom light as a cloud
        the day has turned
                with a fresh breeze from the sea

from somewhere I've acquired a small sail
    striped candy red and white
    fixed to the mast like a flag and billowing
        like the skirts of a parachute
        I feel its sudden tug as it pulls me upward
            hauled along by the wind

higher than ever higher than a kite
    the world reels out below me
    I am soaring solo over the suburbs
            drawn by the salty current a glitter of hail

        towards the city blinking in its mist
            coming clearer with each breath

Steering by the Stars

Nobody steers by starlight any more:
we're too clever for that

we've packed the stars away
in the dusty dark

turned the key in the lock.
Eyes down, we study our instruments

measuring our location
without benefit of heaven

the beasts above us, the ones
with fiery faces

blotted out by light.
We have banished night from the world

who needs it? It belongs
out there with the past

with the star names
of the Magi, who saw

the eyes of the Bull and said:
Aldebaran. Elnath..

Dubhe they said, and *Alioth*
and *Albaid*, the haunches of the Bear.

From the East, a long slow caravan
sets out across the desert

ships navigate the wastes
of the open ocean

and in the empyrean a blaze
of beings journeying

along with them, and Pegasus
is beating his four wings:

Scheat, Markab, Algenib, Alpheratz.
Heroes of old, the Archer

his bow stretched *Nunki* to *Kaus*
and the Hunter with the jewels

in his belt: *Alnilam,*
Rigel and *Betelgeuse* and *Bellatrix.*

In our age they glimmer wearily:
the Hunter with his dogs

Sirius and *Procyon* is redundant
eating burgers, watching Sky TV.

But the old names still resound
like incantations, syllables

of power. Just say it: *Acamar* –
a breath of incense on the night air.

Here are the citadels and palaces:
Alphecca, Al'Nair

Zuben'ubi, Tower of Justice.
Ankaa, the burning Phoenix.

And then the warriors:
Kochab, Polaris, Menkent, Rigilkent

conjured from their strongholds
in the hills, armed with their scimitars –

Schedar. Shaula. Enif.
The fixed stars. They flash crimson

gold and purple, sapphire, emerald.
They spin and twirl, coming to life, pulsating –

we're being watched, the pressure of their gaze
stinging our scalps like rain.

And now the summoning-spell
the words of sorcery:

Mirfak. Denebola.
That's when we all look up.

The Blessing

In this house at dawn
as the first plume of light
brushes the windows

something stirs
in the blind shadows
where sleep has roosted

all night, and moves around
corners, through doors: a creak
on the stairs, a murmur

of water in the plumbing
and a feathery sound
from the dust, a shuffle of quills.

After hours lying dry
and locked in wakefulness,
this hour between dark and day

with its pale glimmer dissolves
the threads that bind you
taut, so they melt at last

and drifting you hear the house wake
around you and preen itself
discreetly, a passing rustle

that shakes and settles
into its morning pattern:
a beady watchfulness

taking over, making it possible
to lie back and let sleep
carry you where it will

while a downy radiance
slowly fills, and unfurls
through the room as you slip past.

My Father Swimming

for Gareth and Anabel

1

In the cold sea his body
slid like a warm knife,
softened the water's slab
coming up buttery
and sleek, with the green
tumbling and rolling off his skin.

His arms flung out to grasp
one handful then another
of solid swell, held all
in a broad embrace
face buried in the foam
blinded with salt. He loved
the pressure of its tongue,
a pearl flicker running over him

like light. And lifting
his head broke the air
into splinters that spun and shone:
sky and land one swinging bright
transparency. No sound
but the red drum of his heart –
all senses drowned
save touch: the sun's hand
smoothing his back and the surface
of the sea. He'd forgotten me

but I was there too, perched
in the rocks stacked like houses
or smoothskinned animals
flushed with heat, sparked with mica;
glad to be high and dry and watching him.

They called it *The Tank*:
this scoop in the cove
granite walled, where the sea funnelled

and boomed, then lingered
pushing at rafts of weed.
Beyond, the Atlantic roared
and fell on the land.
Down here the currents
spread their webbed fingers, tugged
their nets. He felt the cords
loosen, and kicked free.

2

My father's affair with the sea
almost broke my mother:
always dragging us to some shore or other
some windswept headland
our faces whipped with spray.
His eyes the same blue-grey, the same distance.

Twenty years before, in the war –
a ship of prisoners, torpedoed
blew apart, spilled its guts, oil,
dying men, their captors.
My father swam all day
all night. His life fell away
with the ship, left him clean
of past and future, just a swimming creature
lost in the vast glitter,
the ocean's mirror
hung in deep space, swaying.

The friend he tried to save
stopped moving, became dead
weight, and slipped down.
My father would not drown,
the sea loved him.
He lay back, and rocked
like flotsam, cradled in brine.
Swimming to live, floating
an imprint on his cells
that one day would be mine.

At dawn he reached an island.
Fishermen hauled him in
gently, and turned him over.
This was his great adventure.
He never spoke of the captivity
that ground him to a shell:
on broken feet still walking,
still believing that the sea saved him
for coming home somehow.

3

He never taught us to swim.
We taught ourselves, after school
in the public pool
floundering around the shallow end.
The water seared my eyes
with chlorine stink, I disliked it,
the yammering din, the big kids
shoving, barrelling in.

The sea was wild. It swept
my feet from under me, it thundered
over my head, filling my mouth with iron
the taste of blood; it slammed
against me with the weight of the whole world.

But to reach down with my feet
into a void: that was fear
of a different order, feeling death
close over me. So I watched my father
swimming with held breath,
his body blurred
to a paperweight feather
in a sea solid as glass;
until he rose, expanding
toward the surface, smashed through it,
took flesh again, and laughed.

It was the land that killed him.
The long, dry years

grew dense inside him
to an end that was ordinary –
landlocked, and slow.
The tide inched back and left
nothing but a shell, a carapace.
That shrunken face
in the coffin was not him:

he was off somewhere, away
swimming perhaps, with long
and easy strokes, carried
out to a shoreless space
where I cannot follow.

Persephone

1

I have been in the woods.
I know what goes on there.

To enter I must cover myself with moss
muffle my shoes in fur
and practise breathing a different mix of air,

closing the gate behind me.
I am observed by lifeforms
with and without eyes:
blunt nudge of fungi in my direction,

insects with crowded lenses,
the radar of trees. Each footstep
disturbs a city; each heartbeat
releases consciousness for their inspection.

From every wood I take away with me
in miniature a whole forest
impressed on the underside of my skin.
The mud, the twigs are itching

just so I don't forget
out here in the present daylight
what lives in the shade,

what will spring up whenever I sink a spade
in garden soil and strike roots.

2

You wouldn't think it possible to forget
the footsteps following
down the track from the chalk ridge heavy with summer

me with my schoolbag mitching
away with the birds

down the long tunnel of the trees,
and then what happened when the steps grew closer –

but I did, I forgot it all
buried it in the woods
under a heap of leafmould and bramble scrub.

I fell asleep under the hedgebank
burrowed in damp sand

and woke in a different land
treeless, anonymous,
changing my face in a mirror,
rubbing dirt from my knees

and in my mouth the remnants
of scarlet pulp and seeds.

3

The smell of the man the worst
terror worse than fox-stink
or caged beasts in the lion house

his own fear white in his eyes
and his hands shaking

worse than the gag of earth
and the fists that pummelled

Now I know the dread of the wild
creature who scents the hunter
on a small shift of wind

4

My first wood was the pinewood by our house
that heaved its bulk in a flurry of needles,

the tousled heads of trees, their stripped torsos
rising all around us as we climbed

from the frontier of the lawn up into silence
and resinous air. I and my little brother

alone collecting pinecones, scrambling
through the bracken, in the cobwebby light

the needle drifts, the cones with their open petals
dry as shells in our hands, the clumps of heather;

and once in midsummer dusk I saw from my window
a freckled deer with her fawn step over the threshold

into the shadows following our tracks
to the otherworld, until they disappeared.

5

Down in the undergrowth I became a bird:
I leapt up able to fly

scattering bits of stick and dead woodlice
and flakes of bark and leafdust.

Far below the sound of a voice shrieking
while I was perched on a twig
my face hidden in oakleaves

until my murderer blundered away uphill
and the trees swallowed him.

I sped on my new wings over stones and roots
to the hill foot, and I was light
and brilliant as a particle of sun

as I passed the great yew with her many children
electricity on the run

and over the railway I was a blur of feathers,
a tremor through the foxglove pinnacles
and the gate clanged after me and I was gone.

6

After descent, I hope for resurrection –
already
it's happening piecemeal

finger by finger
tooth by lip by hair.
In fact I am almost there:

daily I make myself
reassemble
flesh from the close-packed earth.

And this is labour,
building layer on layer
extricating myself from the tree-shadows.

Slowly, there are changes:
the pain in my neck has gone
that came from clenching myself against the blows.

One day my head will clear
and the last cuts will close.

7

I have been in the woods –
the dancing-floor of the beechwood, its maze of pillars,

wet tangle of a Welsh wood, never far
from the sound of water,

Boskenna Wood with its boulders
and the sea seething through,

the wood where I wandered lost
among darkening yew,

and the wood with a well in its heart,
the spice of ground-ivy
where something made paths.

Every wood I enter I cloak myself
in a dun pelt with pricked ears
and far-spaced eyes

stepping high and gently probing
between the trees,

my fine-tuned fibres crackling
and humming all over my body

picking up scraps of words,
a scrambled undertow of conversation
or maybe a flicker of music
coaxing me sideways off the beaten track,

never afraid but always curious
and watchful for what might come
out of the crumpled ground to claim me back.

A Lap of Apples

Looking for drowned apples
sunk in October seagrass
wet and salt with rot

I wonder what I'll find
in the rooty shade –

firm fruit just slit its skin
oozing white sugar-foam
bruised thumbprints still new,

drill-hole of a bird's bill,
all muddy but edible –

or pretenders laid
squat on a brown soft bloom
or a hollow woodlice home

or worse, those that lurk
under my shoes
blackened as leather balls

grenades in the dew.

A damp trawl nets some
sound ones, plus a few
hangers-on from the trees

to add to the store. Daily
the box fills, and the scent
of apple-ferment rises

cries *eat me* – peel, core,
make pies, make crumbles,

jelly rose glow, sweet
pulp to bag and freeze
and wine, wine......

But what if I don't have time
to deal with this glut?

I'm not the first to know
guilt over apples, regret
over all that's spoiled

all that tumbles into waste.
Did Eve and Adam lose
Eden the day they said

Such a pity this tree's unused!
Let's put this lot
to work for us – in their leafy aprons
bagging up windfalls?

Well if I know God She's no
housewife, She'd rather dance
than sit with a lap of apples.

Slattern, She'll let the mess
take care of itself; which of course
it does – the leaves, the fruit

the lives all fallen
into rich mulch.

Inside

for the Dark Age woman found in the dunes, Co. Donegal

However I appeared
after all these years
it's my inside that's endured

my inner self revealed
as armour, hard
and light and unpeeled

with my life rubbed off
in the sand, the soft
stuff melted, spindrift

web of nerves thrown
to the seawind, gone.
I am pared down to bone.

All my links are unfastened
like a necklace lost
in the dunes and darkened

to potsherd, woodcore.
Good craftwork, the jaw's
carved rack, the scapular

the bentwood tibia,
each ivory finger.
Here's the cracked spar

of my breast, the ribstaves
worked loose, and the cradle
that rocked my babes

is like a blown flower.
The skull is a door
that leads nowhere any more.

But my spine is winged:
now it's a kitestring
uncoiled, a garland,

a skein of moths, a flight
of stairs, a rope, an exit
through the labyrinth of night.

The Badge

Finding myself after nights of grief and dread
in a room full of rainy light
knife in my hand, no-one can do this for me,
I prepare for the ceremony:

I am about to join the community
of those who have removed and replaced their heads.

Cutting it off is easy, I feel no pain,
what's difficult is finding the thing again
wherever on the carpet it's rolled to.

Headless, but I see with shadow-sight
a fluid shudder of colours, images
which will soon falter and disintegrate
unless I reattach my head quickly

and I must do it quickly, it's not too late
while nerves and flesh are still living.

I'm trembling cold and bright
as a knife-edge, I feel high
and light as you do when shrugging off a pack
you've slogged under for miles. And there

on the floor it lies, I recognise the hair
tumbled and black, the face
turned mercifully aside, a glimpse of cheek and brow

that's mine all right so I take it,
lift it like a warm and weighty stone
up to my neck and steady it in place.

I must wait now while vein and bone
and fibres knit together,
motionless in case it all untethers
as round me the others gather

praising, giving me space. Thin fluid
oozes from the join – is this normal? They nod
yes, yes, don't worry, it's healing.

My lover wants to hug me, and I say no
not yet, this is still too new

but he leads me to a seat beneath the window
plump with purple cushions, he kisses me
and promises he won't disturb my head

which balances on its stem
like a flower just opened.

As he enters me I touch my neck
very softly and think of the scar I'll have,
the badge of those who've lost their heads and regained them

a fine red necklace, indelible thread.

Reynardine

'And if by chance you look for me, by chance you'll not me find:
For I'll be in my green castle – enquire for Reynardine' (Trad.)

There was a time it dangled with her clothes
denned in the soft folds
between silk and wool, a touch of animal;

when it was the sly face in the wardrobe
peering from the slot
of a half-open door to whisper to me

from its dry mouth with the black ribbon lips
clamped on tooth slivers,
slant-toed feet stepping through thickets of coats

scuff, scrabble of claws on the bedroom floor
the red shape coming,
a nip of teeth on my neck before I woke.

There was a time my mother wore the fox
over her shoulder
her relic, dated as stays, from a lost age,

with glassy eyes and ears like shrivelled pods
flat to the wedge head
that grinned and nodded at me behind her back.

The figure wavers, dim and towering:
a whiff of camphor,
Nuits de Paris, and cats; the neat paws dancing;

an empty skin, boneless banner of fur
bodiless but wise
keeping an eye on me from the shadow side.

Gently now with the poor tattered bundle:
that sleek seducer
from the pungent woods reduced at last to this.

Snow Story

(for Anne Cluysenaar)

Snowfall has rounded the hills
drawing them nearer
plumping them like mounds in a picture book
like the bowed heads of beasts

grazing in spindle thickets
wreathed in cloudy breath

So she pulls on her boots and takes her coat
and goes out to the cold
shutting her door on grief with no backward look

Her steps creaking gently on the snow
the distant muffled rumble of a plane
these are the only sounds

until she reaches the border of the wood
that crackles with silence and the soft
thud of snow from its branches
a rustle from its heart

But the hind is started:
a sideways glimmer
against the crossed shadow of birch and pine
white as heraldry

white as the white hart in a tapestry
or the innsigns only without its chain
and its golden crown

glancing with the eyes of someone known
from the other side of death

Then with a pale flicker the creature's gone
extinguished to a blank on the retina
leaving the woman frowning in the sun

Nervously she stumps among the brambles
scanning the ground for symbols

and edged in ice she finds
two double slots pressed deep
where the hind leapt the hedge

Now she can turn her back
on the wood and trudge homeward
along the printed track

glad for the evidence of a beast's weight
carried on slender feet

New Poems

A Jungle Tale

It's the last day of term and I'm in the hall with the other school leavers. We are seated at the front, in the place of honour, the rest of the school a breathing sea at our backs. We sit with hands folded on maroon pleated skirts, our knees pressed together, facing the stage.

Our headmistress stands clothed in oldfashioned black with a slim starched wimple, addressing us in clear yet sonorous tones. She is praising us older girls on the threshold of the world. She cites our school achievements. One by one she calls us to the stage and presents us each with a book.

Now it's my turn and I ascend the steps and walk across to her and receive my copy. It's a collection of stories, traditional tales, and all the illustrations have been drawn by us, the members of my class.

Back in my seat, I am astounded. When did I take a fine pencil and sketch out these designs? Try as I might, I can't recall the sensation of the brush between my fingers, the glow of colour on its tip, the vivid array of paints, chrome yellow, rose madder, crimson lake. The pictures are intricate, lovely, and I have no recollection of making them. Yet here they are.

Years have passed. The book was put aside with other remnants, folded in the dark. Now I've rediscovered it, and wondering I turn the half-remembered, unfamiliar pages. I show them to my children, my husband, my friends. My name is there in black and white. Can I really have forgotten so completely?

Which is your story? asks a friend, and I point to a jungle tale. My illustration shows a leopard sinuous among treetrunks, the dappled light revealing other creatures emerging from the leaves: monkeys, snakes, brightwinged birds. I confess that I know nothing about these artworks.

The admission fills me with fear. I am a stranger to myself. I no longer recognise my own footsteps.

But what wonderful artists we were, we girls, at that age! Gradually I relinquish my confusion and allow pride and pleasure to fill me like a spring that pours into a mossy basin in the forest's heart. Birds call and shriek and rustle in the canopy. I sit and rest my spine against the deep olive stem of a tree, and the spring water tastes sweet and stony in my mouth. Sunlight ruffles the pages of my book.

Mute Swan

The wild swan draws near to the forest.
Perhaps she may find a flat branch.   (I Ching: Hexagram 53)

Dusk gathers; the swan beats her wings
slowly against the rain.
She has flown from the lake to the reedbeds,
she has flown from the reeds to the high plain.

She fell among hunters and thieves
and her mate was lost.
For three years she wandered, searching.

At last she draws near to the forest
and a roosting-place.
Light glances and drips from her feathers
as the sun dips low.

Her wings make a humming sound,
a tune she sings over and over
as she enters the trees:

tomorrow in the wind
on her way to the summit
she may find the words.

The Little Hours

Prime

A Kind of Purgatory

Last night I dreamt we were attempting Heaven
(me and my crowd of otherselves):
leaping, flailing, struggling to rise
through a flat murk with no landmarks,

and I remember thinking *we've been through*
the dying bit, and that was trouble enough –
so why is this so hard? Exhaustion seeping
into my limbs like cold sea water.

I wouldn't give up though, gathering myself
for one more lunge and spring.

Lent is a time to grapple with
death and the last things –
those who fall back within sight
of the sun's return, new shoots blackened by frost –

the fast, the hungry gap. It's how it hurts
most at the edge, almost there,
the final mile; it's how the earth labours
at life (once more, once more),
till something green emerges.

And now at last it's time to look up as the sky
lifts and widens, to venture
out in the harsh bright wind,

and see where primroses have colonised
a damp forgotten corner by the wall,
clustered hopeful faces risen through grass;

where birds dart through, without effort,
our weighty atmosphere:

their Heaven achieved, arrived at.

Sea View

The sea from here looks higher than the land:
raised like a curtain
of fine gauze waters, pearly weft
stretched taut and still
across the horizon line

between here and elsewhere.
The land slants down, leans sideways
into the wind that blows always
in this place, on the edge

of the earth. Beyond the sea screen
everything falls away.
That's how it feels today:
the world piled up at my back
like memory

and before me just this blank
sky, the thin worn-out hedge
tossed on the breeze, and the barrier of sea.

Well I can't go back, I'm here now
with my face turned outward
and the sea lifted high
like a banner over me.

The world's upside down and my heart's
in my mouth, and the standing wave's about to
break, and soon the curtain will fly

open and what's beyond will rush
in and swirl and climb to where I stand –

and I'm ready, come what may.
This shore, and a new day:
it's not a bad place to be.

Comfort in Blackthorn
(for Adrian May)

This is what I know about blackthorn.
How bravely it flowers

on naked twigs, on swept grey days
as March winds shake the glitter from its spines;

how it foams in the hedgerows:
cold starry blooms
with gold eyes, watching

for something winged to alight,
for some glimpse of spring.

And how it has a reputation
for strife; how fierce it is
in the gap, such a strong defender
brandishing its spears.
Its wood is good for cudgels.

How it is called in France
'Mother of the Wood' –

but a wild mother
dark-clawed as any fox

whose milk nourishes sloes
that make your tongue pucker.

But even here, there's comfort:
they bring forth saliva.
A tip for thirsty travellers: hold a sloe in your mouth.

And of course, sloes pricked and sugared
and steeped in gin, for Christmas.
Sloe wine too; my speciality

when I can gather enough. It tastes
of blood of the wood, it's the wine

Christ made at Cana, ripe
with magic, bruised at the heart.

Knowledge of blackthorn is rare.
Its small blunt rounded leaves
go unpraised, unnoticed.

What comfort we find there
is a wayside delight
in what flourishes unseen, in odd corners,

and out of grief, out of winter
what twists to life.

Terce

Chorus

A warm spell in May
conjures green from the trees
so everywhere you look, there it is:

spring, that late arrival.

Here it is now, opposite the church
in George Street, a small leaved birch

in a courtyard, putting out its flags,
its soft green tongues.

Across the valley the sloping
woods are furred with life
wide-awake and brimming

with countless leafy tongues
tasting the sunlight
lapping the moistened air:

a chorus of leaves in full song
beyond our range of hearing –

or in conversation, all talking at once.

Whatever it is they say or sing, it must be
joyous – or so it seems to me

as I wander into town with my ears ringing
and music prickling the space between
each built object from the wide-open mouths

of all the new shoots –
a running loop, repeating endlessly:

a concert, given for free.

The Innocent Hare

(Pennant Melangell)
for Norman Schwenk

Poor Puss is running with the dogs
in the sunrise all thick with May dew,
poor Puss with her heart clamouring
blood pumping the long muscles of her thighs

her eyes staring behind at death
hot on her trail with yelps and yammering,
her eyes full of green and hawthorn
open to each spark and flutter of life.

All last night she grazed on the mountain
moonlight silvering her closecropped fur,

all last night she leapt in the grasses
creeping at dawn to her shallow and thorny set

But the hunt is up and she is bounding
over the scree and down to the valley,
the hunt is up and she steers and weaves
through bog and bracken guided by Tanat's stream

following the cool voice of water
rinsing her throat with dappled promises,

following the damp smell of cresses
teasing her ears with secrets and shadowing

So when the hunter comes to the quiet place
his dogs fled scattered and searching,

when the hunter comes to the holy well
all he sees is a young woman kneeling

innocent and dressed in plain grey
her hood thrown over her and slender hands
innocently upraised to praise the day –
O great wide wonderful beautiful World she prays.

Some say the hare is hid beneath my apron
the bonny hare crouched there
under my skirts she smiles, and whoever dares
to lift my shining veil will be struck to stone.

Honey-gold the grove in sunlight

where the hunter stands entranced
by the honey-gold of her hair
and by the curling waters in the pool.

Sweet Puss is flown and gone
underneath and hidden from our eyes,
sweet Puss is lying low in the hollows

of the earth all dressed for the pilgrimage of spring.

(*In many of the traditional songs that tell of the hunting of the hare, the hare is referred to as 'Puss'*)

The Way to the Well

(St. Aelhaern's Well, Gwynedd)

Having gone the wrong way, we found the right way
to the well, past the school with its bell
announcing the end of playtime.

Having seen the wrong thing, we did the right thing,
fished out the clutter – the usual plastic bag
and a stained nylon cloth in place of a pilgrim's rag –

with cheerful reverence at the little spring,
paying attention to the way the rill
ran through its stone basin beneath the hill

into an ugly culvert. We performed all
the right rituals: blessed our faces
with water, and praised the ferns who bowed

as if kneeling and drinking, who curled their fronds
like hands; and invoked the saint
of forgotten places. Then for the ceremony

of the holy photograph we sat on the healing-stone
and smiled. To conclude the rite,
a wish, and an offering of something bright:

a coin tucked into the mossy crevices,
a nod to the watchful ash-tree

in the hedgerow. We walked back past the bungalows
down the zigzag street to the car. Whatever ill

that well is good for, or what sad complaint,
we left in that scoop by the roadside

washed clean, an invisible cloth
hung out on a branch to dry. And it felt good,
having followed sense, and done all the things we should.

Now let the well give its answer, as it will;
as the pilgrims prayed it would.

Sext

Considering the World
(for my mother, died 04.05.2007)

When I consider the world…
I know well
That leaving it will be sad…
('Quant ay lomon consirat' – pilgrims' song, Montserrat)

When I told you that the hedges
are fat with whitethorn
and how the chestnut candles are all lit

you sighed, and shut your eyes,
as if in sorrow to be missing it.

The bluebells that I brought you from my garden
already softening, bending their heads.

Beyond the grubby window of the ward
sun flared, and struck the hummocks of the roof,
with not a blade of green visible.

Holding your hand, the warmth of your grip,
its firmness. You didn't want to let anything go.

But the flesh of your arm, so frail,
petal-soft; and your stricken tongue
trying to make the words work: all we left unsaid.

It was you who showed the world to me,
its feasts and flowers
and creatures. You were my first world.

Remember how you lifted me from sleep
to hear the nightingale? Wild strawberries

you placed in my mouth; the buttercups you held
beneath my chin. Now I want

to bring the world to you, here in your bed,
gathered in your arms, a last gift.

And I wonder, is it lost to you? Or is it found
instead? Not broken, but complete,
bursting with may and birdsong

as you enter with pilgrim feet
the interior of every green thing,

each birdwing, sunmote, raindrop,
the summer of the dead.

Hind's Feet
(for Michael)

He maketh my feet like hinds' feet
and setteth me upon my high places.

Like hinds' feet, narrow and cleft,
with ankles coiled and sprung
for the dancing, for bounding

over rocks and leaping through trees,
for running up slopes and pivoting
on the summit: not like my feet at all

heavy-shod, broad and splayed
for the trudge along pavements,
the plod over tarmac, the march

upstairs and down. My humble feet
thickset to keep me rooted to the ground
aren't used to teetering,

the tiptoe stance of deer, the high
heeled strut, the ballet pirouette,
the toe-hold climb, the long jump.

I'm not good with heights, they make my palms
prickle and weaken my knees:
I need something to cling to. Yet love

has lifted me out of my sad
stiff self and for reasons best known
has set me here in the uplands,

in a wild and far-flung place
full of cloud and heather –
no shelter from changing weather.

Now lightfoot I wander,
and lift my head to the wind
to listen for its direction.

The voice of the Lord shaketh the wilderness…
The voice of the Lord maketh the hinds to calve,
and strippeth the forests bare.

The trail I leave is slender, open
and curved like petals, female
as the horns of the moon.
                (Psalm 18; Psalm 29)

A Flock of Young Birds
for Bob Needs, i.m. Shirley Needs

Something of me, a remnant
enclosed in a little box
tucked away in the rosy earth:

yes, that dear dust, precious
stuff from the breathing body
that flourished and grew from my birth –

while you who loved me gather
around that trace of me,
remember, mourn and pray

on this gentle August day of sun and breeze.

How can I tell you now
how much I love, how happy
I am? How here, how near, how free?

Now in this summer tree
among the leaves, the light,
the webs and spiderlings, the stray bees,

I call these birds to sing that song for me.

None

Like Them That Dream
i.m. Anne Cluysenaar 1.11.14
They that sowed in tears will sing when they reap (Psalm 126)

All your journeys led to your final day.
A day full of sun: the last of summer waving
farewell as it dawdled over the hills,
fingered the fading leaves and let them fall,

strolled along streets and sideroads,
glancing in our gardens
at papery hydrangeas and pale pinched roses,
sliding round corners

to creep in windows and splash warm light on a wall,
deepening all colour. One last, long note
at the end of a symphony. That afternoon

I got the mower out, the manual one I use,
and shoved its blades through damp grass.
The last cut of the year. It snagged and stalled
and chewed up chunks of earth but I persevered:

this, I sensed, would be the last chance. Last chance
to gather husks from the bean canes

and clear the rotting apples from the path,
and weed the veg beds ready for winter planting.

How did you spend your day at the little farm?
With the animals, standing with them in the shade
by the forest eaves? In the kitchen, looking out to the sun,
planning for winter? Thinking of spring, of poems?

Forever looking forward, that's what we do
while we keep breathing and pumping the blood around:
setting out for the future moment, the next hard thing
till the future stops. *Carrying seed for the sowing.*
We shall be *like them that dream*

when our captivity shall be *turned again*
like a stream diverted, surprisingly
and all at once, flowing now in a new direction
into the dry ground, into the empty spaces –

and yes, suddenly facing another way
we'll see what the departing summer sees
as it slips from the hilltop and the rocky places:
the whole world rolling backwards, away from us.

You left the world to its motion, not intending
to leave, but always ready to start. Joining
the tail-end of the harvest celebration –
weeping, singing, carrying your sheaves.

The Science of Magnetism
"We are bubbles of earth! Bubbles of earth! Bubbles of earth!"
(Flora Thompson: Lark Rise)

Now we know the Earth is a winged being,
its molten heart always beating:
a heart of iron, plunged in terrible heat,
the inner sun, a bloodred boiling furnace

with a magnetic pulse that we can measure
in the still rocks and fired clays
cooled from the kiln, or in the needle that wavers
Northward. Its body hums with electricity,

the crackle of life, a breathing out from the South
and inward at the North, an astral plume
of fluid particles, in skirts that fly up
and over, in webs of glowing matter
through which the planet twirls like a Sufi dancer,
or like a moth resplendent in her veils.

Invisible, this field, and magical,
yet fiercely physical, and explicable by numbers:
all thoughts, all stones, all hearts, all cells
spun in the Earth's cocoon. In its charged glow

we see ourselves, small bodies radiating
light from a fiery centre. And as we hold each other
we are two worlds colliding skin to skin
and intermingling, two tiny earth bubbles

floating on the current that's shaping us,
buoyed up by the polarities of love.

An Early Herbal

Gold beneath the chin.
Each flower a sun
plucked from the meadow
held between finger and thumb

come near, come here
a glow on the skin.

Daisies, their frail stems
beneath our fingernails:
to slit without breaking,
threading a chain –

frilled crown and necklace,
the cow-smell of their petals.

He loves me, loves me not.

The tough ribbed stalks
of plantain, a loop
for the perfect shot,

or a bracelet plait,
the brown heads nodding
circled with stars.
Cherries hooked over ears.

All the long grass games:
tunnels, blade-whistles:
cuts bound with spider-silk.

Weaving our birds-nests
lined with moss and trefoil,
though the birds never came –

blown time from dandelions,
our fingers brown and tacky
with bitter milk.

We'd crawl for hours
hunting four-leaved clover;

we'd gather together
sloeberries, rosehips
and polished haws, and acorns,
their goblets spilling over
with river-water –

a fairy feast, offered
in a tree's hollow slot.

Dipping our finger-ends
into foxgloves:

their damp,
their velvet mouths.

Scattering grass-seed
to cling in our hair:
a *bunch of flowers*, pinched up
from the stem, stripped bare.

I can still tell, from the grass-heads,
which will pull clean
from their sheaths and taste sweet.
That rush of green.

In fall, leaf-piles, peltings,
conkers, and twirling
sycamore wings,

forbidden bonfires,
sucking smoke in thick swirls
from elder-pipes,
spluttering, choking.

We'd guzzle blackberries
till we felt purple-sick –
cracked cobs with our teeth.

Pulled from the hedgerows
our props and oracles:

our futures in plumstones,
beggar-man or thief.

Enchanted willow-wands
waved by imperious girls:
I must be princess,
this flower is lucky –

the rules that we forgot.
We'd say, *Do you like butter?*
our faces close together.
He loves me, loves me not.

Compline

Secret

Small movements in the lavender.
Bees about their business:
the secret of honey
that they keep to themselves.

Where my favourite boulder
has slipped a little further
into the river –
new washed moss

and all the hidden creatures
beneath, plunged deeper,
breathing dissolved air.

Walking at night
in summer under the trees
smothered in darkness

while an owl cries
sharp and softly
from its fortress of leaves.

The pressure of your arm
around my waist:

the road ahead invisible,
the scent of flowers arriving
from an unknown place.

Moon Talk

On our last night in your attic room
we argued about the moon
as it hung at your window,
debating its progression across the sky.

I leant across your warm flesh
to peer at that slice of light
that dipped in and out of darkness.

Your body was reflected in the glass
sprawled after love

as if flying to greet me
from somewhere beyond the stars.

I explained the moon to you:
how newly it follows the sun
caught like a barb at its sinking
beneath the rim of the world,

then how it breaks free and flowers
and lags behind, night by night,
going its own way,
until at last we see the moon by day.

You laughed, and questioned how I'd know
this astronomy, this witchcraft.

Well, you started the moon-talk
months ago, when you told me how it shone
full on your bed, how you wanted me
beside you bathed in moonlight.

I imagined that light on your skin
turning you silver, and my hands on you
like two clouds, pale as frost.

That was your dream, your moon –
it belongs to you, you know its wanderings
and shape-shiftings, its voyages through space.

I've drawn you down to me
but I can't hold you:
though you love me still you go from me
over and over, cosmic visitor.

But there'll be other rooms, when you've walked down
those stairs for the last time,
other windows for the moon to enter,

where we'll lie down together;
where we'll study the shifting weather,
where the dream will not be lost.

Valentine's Day in the Eastern Valley

Feels like spring today, the sun emerging
from her cave, a scatter of gold on the rooftops,
daffodils spiking the grass as I steer
past the school, past the fortress church, downhill

to the traffic lights. Waiting on red
I watch, as always, the opposite woods
rising steep from the river. Now they flush dark
purple with new buds, wine-dipped.

The lights flick green, and I turn
left, and follow the valley's shabby heels
through diminishing straggles of town
as it strides up the mountain, gathering ground.

Trees crowd close to the road, and among
them I catch odd flickers and slips
of shadow, a feathered glance, the clip of beak
on twig, and the headlong cwm alive

with wings. I remember what day it is: the weddings
of the birds. The seed-birds, the worm-birds,
and the water-birds, and all the birds of prey.
The janglynge pye, the stare, the skornynge jay.

They chatter, whistle, shout, or gently call
in their congregation, sex on their minds,
and the solemn, playful rituals of pairing.
Uninvited, I drive by, carrying my heart

in silence. The woods fall back, and the hilltop
town, and the shattered ironworks. The road bends
wearily to the mountain. The sky opens up
around me. Ragged sheep, with windtorn wool,

a lonely buzzard, searching. And now, and now –
the vision of peaks, the glorious plunge, today
all ruffled in fogbanks, a Chinese
landscape, rolled in pearl, the undiscovered

country. There's a car in the layby, a woman
looks out at the view. I drive on down
through trees and cavorting birds, too soon
for spring but I'm almost singing

towards my unromantic rendezvous.

An Eye Test

(for Deborah Kay Davies)

This is your right eye says the girl in white,
priestess of the lenses.

She touches a key, and the monitor reveals
a globe of pink-gold:

a lantern lit from within
hung out in the darkness,
a planet in deep space, sulphurous,

traced with scarlet threads,
with a small cloudy pole.
Your optic nerve she says, pointing.

All images I've seen since my beginning,
countless slides of the world, have passed through

that portal veiled in bright mist:
reversed projections, marvellous

reflections made of light
turned around in my head,

set on their feet again and sent out
through my body as awareness.

Too easy to say *windows of the soul* —
these are tissue and warm fluid

mirror familiars, brown iris ringed
with off-white cornea, framed by my lids'

dark lashes, the delicate skin
that I dab with cream daily:
the same old gaze to my gaze.

Now I must reinvent
the word *eye*, discover its hidden meaning,
having seen this orb seeming

remote as a distant world
etched with rivers of blood;

and I must also find a new word
for *planet*, that celebrates the flesh.

Out there in infinite blackness
are billions of eyes

with everything that is, or was, or will be
seen perfectly, reflected, recognised.

And this is your left eye. Twin globes,
a solar system; then my mind's a sun,

like all those far stars burning.

Facts of Life

(for my children)

They come from Elsewhere.

They arrive exhausted:
so they cry, they sleep.

Through the tunnels of the deep
the winged aeons

they laboured, gathering themselves
into shape as they drew closer:
sailing through time, against the tide of matter

through the snow and crackle
of an untuned channel

tangled in bright filaments of mind,
growing a sphere of light.

Out there, drawing near, coming here –
a humming swarm of them
beelike, cells in a hive:
yet each its own self, alive.

So it was when I looked into your eyes
still filmed with memory
still travelling towards me;

you turned your head, disappointed,
and clutched the air.

I held you tightly, making you aware,
I brought you to yourself;
warm milk entered your belly

and straightaway you started to forget
your journey, the task you must do –

we all forget: each day
settling into the rhythms of the heart,
the body's edges closing, comforting.

Until perhaps years later we awake
to doors shutting softly
inside us, on some dream

immense and true
yet irretrievable,
dissolving even as we reach for it –

in which we almost remembered,
almost knew.

A Long Goodbye

i.m. Tony Padfield

Unravelling

The long unravelling.
The crinkled threads
unzip themselves, and spring free:
bubble and coil, and float
in an airy tangle

of unknit plans.
Colours still sing and burn
as bright as ever but without form
where the pattern's gone:
yellow is only yellow, red is red.

Summer is over, and the trees seal off
their tips and the sap falls
into the root and the leaves
blaze briefly then loosen
and blow away
all, all in a day.

You turn to me and speak,
and lose a word –
a dropped stitch;
an undone leaf.

Unhinged

As if we were doors.
As if our minds were doors
to pass through, knock
and gain admittance.

Needing a good stout frame
to swing from, to and fro,

open and shut:
a tongue-latch, and a lock.

This door has never hung
as it should. You've taken it
from its hinges, planed and scraped
its edges, screwed it back:
still it sticks, and the brass knob
rattles. You said you'd fix it

but now you can't be troubled
by tasks and tools, and I
don't have time or skills.

And so I shove it shut and wrench
it open, feeling my own

frame loosen,
sensing the structure buckle
under strain –

nothing to keep the fear
and the fury from flying out, though I clench
my teeth till my jaw aches –

nothing to keep the dark
from seeping in
round the edges, through the gaps:

black wind, and cold rain.

A Separate Reality

I come into the 'dream'
by breaking out of the back garden
into the lane. I don't like
whatever is going on there.

He'd come out because he thought there were
builders in every room

clambering over the furniture, some using ladders,
sloshing paint around, banging in nails;

doing what should be my job.
No-one replied to his questions.

Was he still in his own home,
or had he stumbled somehow
into someone else's life? But he can't remember.

He must find a police station, *to throw myself*
on their mercy, to find where I live.
Wisely, he's brought some possessions:
just a few clothes, and a rucksack.

I must keep a brave face on things
he tells himself, as he stumbles down the lane -
in case he should get *arrested*
for being in the wrong house.

And the rucksack is now so heavy! A crushing load.
This rough track turns out to be uphill. After all,
I expected a struggle.

A man bobs out of a garden gate
and disappears again. He decides against
asking this man for directions
as he knows *what's about to happen –*
my head's going out of balance,
backwards this time.

So he has to let go, and fall.

And here's his son, *right on cue,*
picking him up, dusting him down;
ushering me in the direction
of what I must agree with him is my home.

It is summer in the garden,
full of low-flying butterflies.

Into the house they go, through the back kitchen.
It smells of sawn timber, and paint.

He thinks his son is hurrying him along
some narrow corridor.
In the dining room there's a plasterer
balanced mysteriously halfway up the wall.

He can't see how he hangs there:
it makes him nauseous.
Neither of us gets much response when they greet him.

The front room, as he guessed, is full of strangers;
though he recognises his son
among paint stains and plaster smears –
he looks quite the expert.

And there's a young woman who may be his daughter,
though I'm not convinced of that.

Everyone's lounging around
on old mattresses and bedsteads.
Nobody speaks to him.

His son is talking to someone on the phone,
giving a long explanation
of how he rescued Dad from the back lane.

I feel grey with fatigue. I must lie down
and close my eyes. I need to build up
my strength to move out of this space I'm in.

He knows his son has been talking to his mother
– and there's a bit of a feeling
I may be losing my mind.

★

His wife has gone away on a complex journey
to London but the bus has got stuck somewhere.
Numbers of taxi cabs are waiting outside.
The drivers are being looked after in the kitchen.

He has noticed a *striking resemblance*
to his own terraced home:
the safe house where he said goodbye
to his wife yesterday.

I am a man sitting in a film set
drinking someone else's coffee,
wondering if I'll recognise
the other rooms in the house.

When his wife returns next day
things seem almost normal.
The builders have gone away, and the phone works.
Yet he remains *petrified with fear* and longing
to get back to his real home,
unable to ask what has been done to him.

If these episodes (he writes some weeks later)
are a separate Reality that explains
why they have to be entered into.

There are people about –
but they seem like passing clouds.
If I want to enter their space
then I'll have to psyche myself up,
watch my breathing, drink water.

Here (he finishes) *is where I ought to stop,*
to sort out what continuum I'm in,
before the day begins to close in on me.

Hello

After months of silence
struck dumb with the senselessness
of it all, bewildered
by seas of syllables breaking over your head,

now on a hospital bed
washed up like withered flotsam on a rock

left high and dry
with a fumbling tongue,
unable to swallow even a cool drop,

eyes glazed with distance
far out, just too far out
to catch a glimpse of the shore –

all of us still calling you, speaking
to you but for weeks now never expecting
one word from you any more –

this afternoon when I
was weary and numb with watching,

your eyes cleared and you stared at me and said:
"Hello!!"
Distinct, surprised, and slow.

Astonishment in your smile
and delight as I reached
through the waves to grasp your hand,
to haul you back to land.

But the dense dark waters O
the deeps rushed in
and snatched your hand away,

bundled you off before I'd time to say
lovely to have you back and
sorry for everything –

swept back out of earshot, dwindling.

+   +   +

Vigil
21.10.2008

You on your bed on your side with your knees bent, breathing.
Hands clasped around your hollow middle, breathing.

Slender long hands that I loved, now blotched with age,
Blue veins shuffling life-blood, you're still breathing.

Eyes closed against the world, a slice of light
Beneath your lids, you're frowning as you're breathing

From distress or concentration? I ask you this:
You don't answer me, but just keep on breathing.

Lovely oxygen, how we crave it, pull it in –
My own breath widens, deepens, we're both breathing.

You're hot and damp with sweat, you could be running
Or climbing towards a summit, heavy breathing.

Up on our roof years back, you lashed to the chimney
With your old climbing rope, I was barely breathing

As you fixed a wobbly cowl, at ease in the sky
As on a crag, sidestepping the wind and breathing.

You never liked to be still, you are not still now,
But immersed in some mighty task, and breathing, breathing.

The room is dim in lamplight, shadow-filled,
The bed with its rumpled quilt is a nest of breathing.

Long pauses now between breaths, losing strength:
Such a stupendous feat, this work of breathing.

I gather you in my arms and kiss your face.
You open your eyes, breathe in; then you stop breathing.

Rest now, rest now I say *I am here with you* –
My love surrounds you as long as I stay breathing.

The Leaves of Life

O it was under the leaves, and the leaves of life,
I met with virgins seven:
And one of them was Mary mild,
Our Lord's sweet Mother of heaven... (Trad song)

It was under the leaves and the leaves of life –
Sweet mother of heaven, Mary mild
was searching for her child.

Go down they said *into yonder town –*

as once she had searched so many years ago
dumb with panic, through shops and byways
for the boy who'd slipped aside
from her for the business that led him here.

She pressed through the surging mob
as fast as foot could go –

through the shouts and jeers
through the flicker of nightmares
scenting his sweat, blood of her blood.

And it's many the bitter and the grievous tear
from the Virgin's eyes did flow.

He met her there, on the road
all bruised and bowed down,
the world bound to his shoulders,
and raised his head and smiled:

O peace Mother, O peace Mother –

the brave, the terrible, the divine child.

Hens in the Yard

Tynewydd, New Inn, Pencader
Blink once, and you'll miss it:
blink twice, and you may see
a house so small
huddled back from the road
down in the skirts of the village;

something snagged on the edge of your eye
like a fragment of dream, an elf-
shape caught between frames, then gone.

A house shrunk by time
as we grew, and flew away
like moths from a spent cocoon.

Your childhood nested deep
in its stones, a spider tracery,
papery and frail, little breaths of dust
on the roped and turning stairs.

Like a cradle, like a suit of clothes
outgrown, no fitting back in,
discarded; or an old car
stalled in a field, empty-eyed.

I remembered the antique yard
with its careful cobbles, close-set,
stacked like cards, where I knelt in sun
to weed with a knife, happy all afternoon;

not heeding the stares of neighbours
(why don't you just use Roundup?) I'd bend to my task,
ora et labora, greeting each stone.

Or painting the squat broad door
bright as a dandelion; fixing
our handmade window frames
into the deep walls, puttying
in the old wavy panes.

Never go back
they say. Never crush the coiled shell
around the soft-bodied moments
that form a life.
No need to suffer the shock
of thick white gloss
over the varnished sashes,
the yard choked with thistles;

no need to witness the loss
of the wide oak planks in the hall
that we stripped, strata by strata
of wallpapers, down to ancient newsprint,
to smooth and polish with beeswax.

So for years we kept away,
holding the house in a tiny jewelled box
in a chamber of the heart,
stooping to peer through its windows
at vast, unbounded spaces.

Until the other day, when you sent
a photo taken on a homeward journey
of the little house with its yard of clean cobbles
and a fresh-painted door, and flowers
by the gate, and a stack of logs,
and chickens in a pen: two speckled hens
with an ark and a zinc drinker.

No looking-in at the lives
of the new keepers of the hidden rooms
of the cottage made of stone and water
(ceiling-beams from a shipwreck, floor
of rippled slates from a river);

but I reach inside my heart, and draw
out the boxed version and find it whole:
and place it beside my phone
with the image there, with the hens in the yard.

The Side Gate

Wenhaston, Suffolk

As we drove to see the Doom
the fields were lit with September sun
and the sky widened to eternity.

Opening the door of the plain church
the usual well of shadow:
then the painted figures greeted us

in their dewfresh colours,
softened by time and the veil
through which we glimpse that other world.

Christ balanced on his rainbow
robed in red above the saved and damned
(all stripped alike and spindle-limbed in death)

gazed down without surprise as we stood there
blowers-in from our century, you in your blue
T-shirt, me in my jeans.

Caught in that still moment
that separates the loving from the lost,
where Michael stands with his sword
and his Libran scales

dividing past from future
and happiness from pain
our cleverness faded, and silence seemed best.

Like a weaned child upon its mother's breast
I have not gone after mysteries beyond me....
Even so is my soul at rest.

And I wondered, where are we pictured in that scene
on the painted boards? In the mouth
of Hell, or wearing golden crowns?

Now I think we might be those two souls
slipping in at the side gate,
the postern-door of Heaven,

unregarded by St. Peter
in his dignity, just beckoned
through by a minor angel:

not quite believing our luck
has turned, and probably undeserving
of our fate, yet spared by grace

for a share of bliss. Outside
the year was poised
between light and dark, the sun

taking its southbound journey.
We shut the door behind us as we left,
our judgement waiting for a small space

behind us, our lives ahead,
until we join the dead
rainwashed, revealed, like this.

Notes

The Tree Calendar

I wrote this sequence of poems in 1985, one poem every four weeks during the course of the year. It is based on an ancient calendar from Ireland and Wales, in which each 28-day month is named after a tree or important plant. This version of the tree calendar comes from Robert Graves's book *The White Goddess,* which I found intriguing and inspirational when I first read it in my twenties. The initial letters of the tree names also formed the main consonants of the Gaelic alphabet, which emphasises the old northern European link between trees and language. I wrote each poem in its appropriate month, so the sequence also serves as a record of that (unusually wet) year.

Birch/Beth: The first month of the Tree Calendar, beginning after the Winter Solstice. It was customary to sweep out the old year with a birch broom or besom, to make way for the new.

Rowan/Luis: The feast of St. Brigid/Bride/Sant Ffraid takes place during the Rowan month. The great prehistoric deity of Britain and Ireland was also named Brighde/Bride. Her name means "bright" and she was associated with the sun, which is beginning to strengthen in early February. She presided over childbirth and the fertility of flocks, fire and smithcraft, and poetry. The quotation is from the *Carmina Gaedelica,* a record of poems, prayers and incantations from the Hebrides collected by Alexander Carmichael.

Ash/Nion: Here I refer to the god Odin from Norse mythology, whose World Tree Yggdrasil was an ash. At its foot sat the three Norns, old women weaving the web of life and cutting it off at the loom. Odin hung three days and nights from Yggdrasil in order to acquire the secret of the runes, or writing.

Alder/Fearn: In Welsh mythology the alder is associated with the raven or crow, Brân. Alder leaves yield a green dye that was used by outlaws as camouflage. The background to the poem was a storytelling/drama based on the story of Taliesin from the *Mabinogion.*

Willow/Saille: Willow was thought to be an unlucky plant, despite its healing properties (aspirin is derived from willow bark). To wear a garland of willow was a sign that you had been jilted in love.

Hawthorn/Huath: Hawthorn was an extremely potent and magical tree, a fairy tree, hence the ban on cutting it and bringing the blooms into the house.

Oak/Duir: Along with ash and hawthorn, one of the three powerful trees of Britain (and sacred to the Druids of course). This month is at the height of the year, before the sun begins to decline after the summer solstice. Oak leaf wine is actually very pleasant, and tastes like a medium sherry, though not quite as strong.

Holly/Tinne: According to Robert Graves (influenced by Frazer and the *Golden Bough*) early agricultural societies sacrificed their king during this month, in preparation for harvest. So "The holly wears the crown" only for the first half of the year. The month of July is dedicated to the Precious Blood of Christ in traditional Catholicism.

Hazel/Coll: A rainy August visit to North Wales, and the holy well at Clynnog Fawr. I refer to the Welsh and Irish legend of the Well at the World's End, where the Salmon of wisdom dwells, feeding on the nuts falling from the sacred hazel, tree of wisdom, that grows overhead.

Bramble/Muin: The bramble isn't really a tree, but it's the British equivalent to the vine, the original plant for this month. Here is a childhood memory of picking blackberries by a burnt-out ruined manor house, that we were all convinced was haunted of course.

Ivy/Gort: The refrain is from the title of a Chinese festival that occurs during this month. I happened to notice this on a calendar of feasts and festivals from around the world, and the phrase caught my imagination. I also refer to one of the hexagrams of the Chinese oracle *I Ching*: no.23 *Po* (Splitting Apart), which is associated with the late autumn.

Reed/Ngetal: This was such an important plant for thousands of years, being used for thatching and basket making and for many other purposes. A plant growing in water, used to keep the water out.

Elder/Ruis: *Huldre Folk...* These are dangerous woodland beings, deceptively beautiful until they turn their backs, which are said to be hollow and empty. They are particularly associated with elder trees. The verse at the end is an old East Anglian spell, to be said in the unlucky event of cutting an elder tree. A version of it, with a Scandinavian equivalent, is given in Katharine Briggs' *The Hidden People*.

Book of Shadows

This sequence grew from an interest I had in the controversial Renaissance mage, Dominican monk and philosopher Giordano Bruno, born in Nola near Naples in 1548 and burnt at the stake for heresy in 1600. In his early career he became an outstanding practitioner of the Dominican *Ars Memoria* or Art of Memory, which he took in various far-reaching and heterodox directions, until leaving the monastery to pursue his interest in alchemy and the magical arts. Bruno was a prolific writer in his short career, and many of his writings are in the form of poetry. He spent a couple of years in England (1583-6) as chaplain to the French ambassador, and became a well-known figure at the court of Elizabeth I. During his time in England he wrote several of his most interesting works, including his great poetic treatise *De Gli Eroici Furori* (On Heroic Frenzy) which he dedicated to his friend Sir Philip Sidney. Both Bruno and Sidney had links to the Welsh magician Dr. John Dee and his circle. There is some evidence that Shakespeare knew of Bruno and his teachings (see F. Yates: *Giordano Bruno and the Hermetic Tradition* ch. XIX). In fact the name of Giordano Bruno was notorious throughout Europe. He continued to be an important influence on non-establishment thought until about the middle of the seventeenth century, when the new scientific rationalism finally triumphed.

I first became interested in Bruno through reading the novels of the American writer John Crowley, especially his masterpiece *Little, Big* in which Bruno is first mentioned, and *Aegypt* in which Bruno features more directly.

In seeking some kind of structure to build the poems around, I used the Tarot with its 22 'Major Arcana' cards; therefore each poem's number corresponds to one of the cards in the Arcana.

For this Selected Poems I have chosen just a few from the sequence that I feel stand alone without a lot of explanation. The quotes at the beginning of each poem are from Bruno's writings. The full sequence can be read in my collections *Book of Shadows* and *Hummadruz*.

Athene: Athene was the Greek goddess of wisdom, whose symbol was an owl. Bruno's quote at the beginning is taken from the Biblical Book of Wisdom. The Wisdom of God, Who could be equated with the Holy Spirit, is referred to as feminine in the Hebrew scriptures. Athene's owl motif can be traced backed to prehistoric 'eye goddess' representations. The Tarot card is *The Priestess* or *Papess.*

The Inner Artificer: The poem arose from a photograph of a "transgenic" pig developed in the United States in the late 1980s. The embryo pig had been implanted with human growth gene. It grew to an enormous size, but was blind, excessively hairy, sterile, and crippled with arthritis. Pig 6707 was considered a great advance in the science of bioengineering. Transgenic, DNA and transhuman experiments continue of course to this day, and on a worldwide scale on the human immune system through ongoing experimental injections. The Tarot card is *The Empress.*

The Revolving Castle: The title refers to the British goddess Arianrhod, whose name means "silver wheel", the goddess of the stars and the turning heavens. According to the Mabinogion, she is a sorceress dwelling in the Revolving Castle. The spider is associated with her, probably because of its spinning webs. The Greek deity Ariadne, with her spool of yarn and labyrinth, is also associated with the spider, and may have some link with Arianrhod. The Tarot card is *The Wheel of Fortune.*

Alchemy: Alchemy was a respected and more or less acceptable pursuit in Bruno's time, though it had its spiritual dangers. Even in the seventeenth century, the scientist John Newton was a practicing alchemist as well as a firmly believing Christian. In the twentieth century, the psychologist Carl Jung used the symbols of alchemy to describe important transformations in the human psyche. The Tarot card is *Temperance,* classically depicted as an angel pouring liquid from one cup to another.

The Voyager: The Tarot card for this poem is *The Moon.*

Animaculture

Mother Anthony's: "Mother Anthony's Well" is in Mother Anthony's Wood, a mysterious place below Oliver's Castle near Devizes in Wiltshire. When we lived for a while in Wiltshire, my late husband and I discovered the wood, and returned many times trying to find the well. Others have said that they found it quite easily…

Greenland

Out With My Broomstick: This poem came from a dream that I had around the time that my eldest child left home to go to university. For several years I regularly had vivid and amazing dreams; I rarely get them now unfortunately. Many of them inspired poems.

My Father Swimming: My father had Welsh ancestry but was brought up in north Cornwall, where he learned to swim in the sea, at Chapelporth. He joined the Royal Marines when he left school before the Second World War, and served in the Far East. On Christmas Day 1941 he was captured defending Hong Kong, and was a prisoner of the Japanese for the remainder of the war. On 25th September 1942 he was transferred with about 1800 other prisoners from Sham Shiu Po camp in Hong Kong to the *Lisbon Maru* to be shipped to a camp in Japan. On 1st October the ship was struck by an American torpedo. The ship went down the following day, and 1000 prisoners perished. My father managed to escape from the nailed-down hold and swam for several miles till he reached an island, where Chinese fishermen rescued him and cared for him until he was recaptured, and punished severely for his "attempt to escape". He rarely mentioned his wartime experiences, but told us a bit more while he was dying. This tragic incident is recounted in Tony Banham's book *The Sinking of the Lisbon Maru* (Hong Kong University Press, 2006). My poem is included in the book. "The Tank" is a deep tidal pool in St. Loy's Cove, Penwith. This was our local beach when our family lived at Boskenna when I was 10-11 years old. My father died in the early hours of 2nd February 1981, of cancer, aged 67. My poem 'Candlemas' from *The Tree Calendar* recalls the night of his death.

The Badge: This was another dream – one of a few involving heads. Many years later, and after writing this poem, I visited St. Winifred's holy well in North Wales and discovered that, according to her legend, after her head was struck off by her vengeful father, it was reattached by St. Bueno, and for the rest of her life she bore a scar around her neck – like the "fine red necklace" of my dream.

The Little Hours

In the monastic day, following the sixth-century Rule of St. Benedict, there are eight formal periods of communal prayer, based on the Psalms, known as the Monastic Hours or Canonical Hours. The first 'Hour', which occurred shortly after midnight, was Matins. Then at dawn, Lauds. Then Prime shortly after that, Terce at mid-morning, Sext at midday, None mid-afternoon, Vespers at dusk, and Compline before retiring for the night. Matins, Lauds and Vespers were longer, and considered the major Hours: the others were shorter, the 'Little Hours'. Most monastic communities nowadays dispense with the Little Hours, other than Sext or midday prayer: only the more traditional orders keep to the original pattern. The Little Hours celebrate what may be overlooked, sidelined, forgotten, dispensable. Also those moments in the midst of a busy, distracted day, when something touches us, alerts us, draws us out of ourselves.

The poems in this sequence were not written with that in mind, but I used the concept of the Hours while arranging them.

Hinds' Feet: This poem was commissioned for an anthology published in 2011 to coincide with the 400th anniversary of the publication of the King James Version of the Bible (*KJV: Old Text, New Poetry* – Wivenhoe Press) Writers were asked to contribute poems based on text from this translation of the Bible. Contributors include Fleur Adcock, Ian Duhig, Kevin Crossley-Holland, Pauline Stainer and Penelope Shuttle, together with other excellent poets. Thanks to Adrian May and Essex University.

A Long Goodbye

I had been married to Tony for thirty years when he died of Lewy Body Dementia in 2008. From his evident decline in 2003 till well after his death I wrote very little poetry, but the poems in this sequence came from that time.

A Separate Reality: This poem is based on an extraordinary account, written by Tony himself during a more lucid spell, of a disturbing episode that occurred while I was away teaching a poetry course and our son was looking after him at home. The notes he wrote were disjointed, but with his help I arranged them into a more coherent form, always using his exact words. These exact words are the sections in italics in the poem, and the rest of the poem is based on his notes. I think it's an astonishing insight into the mind of someone suffering from this particular condition, which is characterised by hallucinations or waking dreams. Tony was proud of what he had written and told me that he hoped it would be useful in some way in the study of LBD. "A Separate Reality" is the title of one of Carlos Castenada's books. Tony was a big fan of Castenada (though he never indulged in hallucinatory drugs!), and I think one way he had of dealing with his illness was to see it as a portal into another world.

The Leaves of Life: The title of a very old folk song, probably part of a mediaeval mystery play of the Passion. The poem recalls one of the Stations of the Cross, an old Christian devotion on the Passion and death of Christ: the fourth station, in which Jesus meets His mother on the way to Calvary. The lines in italics are from the song.

Acknowledgements

Many of these poems have appeared in the following magazines and journals: *Poetry Wales, New Welsh Review, Planet, Scintilla, Other Poetry, PBS Anthology. National Poetry Competition Anthology, The London Magazine.* Also in the following anthologies from Seren: *Poetry Wales 25 Years* ed. Cary Archard, *Drawing Down the Moon* /*Poetry Wales 40 years* ed. Robert Minhinnick, *Birdsong / Childhood / A Child's Christmas in Wales* ed. Dewi Roberts, *Twentieth Century Anglo-Welsh Poetry* ed. Dannie Abse, *Poet Portraits* ed. Lorraine Bewsey and Anne Price-Owen, *Burning the Bracken / Women's Work / Poems from Pembrokeshire* ed. Amy Wack. And in other anthologies: *Trees Be Company* ed. Angela King and Susan Clifford (Bristol Classical Press 1989), *The Bright Field* ed. Meic Stephens (Carcanet 1991), *The Urgency of Identity* ed. David Lloyd (Triquarterly Books 1994), *The River's Voice* ed. Angela King and Susan Clifford (Green Books 2000), *The Poet's House* ed. Jude Brigley (Pont Poetry 2000), *In een ander licht* (Wagner & Van Santen 2001), *Earth Songs* ed. Peter Abbs (Green Books 2002), *The Pterodactyl's Wing* ed. Richard Gwyn (Parthian 2003), *The Hare That Hides Within* ed. Anne Cluysenaar and Norman Schwenk (Parthian 2004), *Images of Women* ed. Myra Schneider (Arrowhead 2006), *Poetry 1900-2000* ed. Meic Stephens (Parthian 2007), *KJV – Old Text, New Poetry* ed. Joan Norlev Taylor (Wivenhoe Books 2011), *At Time's Edge – Remembering Anne Cluysenaar* ed. Fiona Owen (Vaughan Association 2016).